WORLD
HISTORY SERIES

The Agricultural Revolution

Titles in the World History Series

WORLD
HISTORY SERIES

The Agricultural
Revolution

by
Cathryn J. Long

LUCENT
BOOKS®

THOMSON
─────────✶─────────™
GALE

San Diego • Detroit • New York • San Francisco • Cleveland • New Haven, Conn. • Waterville, Maine • London • Munich

For more information, contact
Lucent Books
27500 Drake Rd.
Farmington Hills, MI 48331-3535
Or you can visit our Internet site at http://www.gale.com

LIBRARY OF CONGRESS CATALOGING-IN-PUBLICATION DATA

Long, Cathryn J.
    The agricultural revolution / by Cathryn J. Long.
        p. cm. — (World history series)
Includes bibliographical references (p.   ).
    ISBN 1-59018-180-8 (hard cover : alk. paper)
    1. Agriculture—Europe—History—Juvenile literature. 2. Agriculture—Technology transfer—Europe—History—Juvenile literature. 3. Agricultural innovations—Europe—History—Juvenile literature. I. Title. II. Series.
    S452.L66 2004
    630'.94—dc22
                                                                    2004010205

Printed in the United States of America

Contents

Foreword

Each year on the first day of school, nearly every history teacher faces the task of explaining why his or her students should study history. One logical answer to this question is that exploring what happened in our past explains how the things we often take for granted—our customs, ideas, and institutions—came to be. As statesman and historian Winston Churchill put it, "Every nation or group of nations has its own tale to tell. Knowledge of the trials and struggles is necessary to all who would comprehend the problems, perils, challenges, and opportunities which confront us today." Thus, a study of history puts modern ideas and institutions in perspective. For example, though the founders of the United States were talented and creative thinkers, they clearly did not invent the concept of democracy. Instead, they adapted some democratic ideas that had originated in ancient Greece and with which the Romans, the British, and others had experimented. An exploration of these cultures, then, reveals their very real connection to us through institutions that continue to shape our daily lives.

Another reason often given for studying history is the idea that lessons exist in the past from which contemporary societies can benefit and learn. This idea, although controversial, has always been an intriguing one for historians. Those who agree that society can benefit from the past often quote philosopher George Santayana's famous statement, "Those who cannot remember the past are condemned to repeat it." Historians who subscribe to Santayana's philosophy believe that, for example, studying the events that led up to the major world wars or other significant historical events would allow society to chart a different and more favorable course in the future.

Just as difficult as convincing students of the importance of studying history is the search for useful and interesting supplementary materials that present historical events in a context that can be easily understood. The volumes in Lucent Books' World History Series attempt to present a broad, balanced, and penetrating view of the march of history. Ancient Egypt's important wars and rulers, for example, are presented against the rich and colorful backdrop of Egyptian religious, social, and cultural developments. The series engages the reader by enhancing historical events with these cultural contexts. For example, in *Ancient Greece*, the text covers the role of women in that society. Slavery is discussed in *The Roman Empire*, as well as how slaves earned their freedom. The numerous and varied aspects of everyday life in these and other societies are explored in each volume of the series. Additionally, the series covers the major political, cultural, and philosophical ideas as the torch of civilization is passed from ancient Mesopotamia and Egypt, through Greece, Rome, Medieval Europe, and other world cultures, to the modern day.

The material in the series is formatted in a thorough, precise, and organized manner. Each volume offers the reader a comprehensive and clearly written overview of an important historical event or period. The topic under discussion is placed in a broad, historical context. For example, *The Italian Renaissance* begins with a discussion of the High Middle Ages and the loss of central control that allowed certain Italian cities to develop artistically. The book ends by looking forward to the Reformation and interpreting the societal changes that grew out of the Renaissance. Thus, students are not only involved in an historical era, but also enveloped by the events leading up to that era and the events following it.

One important and unique feature in the World History Series is the primary and secondary source quotations that richly supplement each volume. These quotes are useful in a number of ways. First, they allow students access to sources they would not normally be exposed to because of the difficulty and obscurity of the original source. The quotations range from interesting anecdotes to farsighted cultural perspectives and are drawn from historical witnesses both past and present. Second, the quotes demonstrate how and where historians themselves derive their information on the past as they strive to reach a consensus on historical events. Lastly, all of the quotes are footnoted, familiarizing students with the citation process and allowing them to verify quotes and/or look up the original source if the quote piques their interest.

Finally, the books in the World History Series provide a detailed launching point for further research. Each book contains a bibliography specifically geared toward student research. A second, annotated bibliography introduces students to all the sources the author consulted when compiling the book. A chronology of important dates gives students an overview, at a glance, of the topic covered. Where applicable, a glossary of terms is included.

In short, the series is designed not only to acquaint readers with the basics of history, but also to make them aware that their lives are a part of an ongoing human saga. Perhaps then they will come to the same realization as famed historian Arnold Toynbee. In his monumental work, *A Study of History*, he wrote about becoming aware of history flowing through him in a mighty current, and of his own life "welling like a wave in the flow of this vast tide."

Important Dates in the History of the Agricultural Revolution

1600s
Private enclosure by large landowners under way in Britain.

1724–1726
Publication of Daniel Defoe's *A Tour Through the Whole Island of Great Britain,* giving much local information about agriculture and the economy.

1730
Rotherham plow patented in Britain.

1767
Arthur Young's first publication of many that explain and promote aspects of the agricultural revolution in Britain.

1760s
First British canals built.

1770
Oliver Goldsmith's poem "The DesertedVillage" reflects feelings against enclosure in Britain.

1793
Board of Agriculture established in Britain to aid improvement; Eli Whitney invents the cotton gin in the United States.

1600	1700	1720	1740	1760	1780	1800

1705
Thomas Newcomen invents the piston steam engine (improved over next one hundred years).

1731
Jethro Tull publishes *Horse Hoeing Husbandry* in Britain.

1772
British parliament removes laws against middlemen in trade.

1786
Andrew Meikle invents a mechanical thresher/winnower in Britain.

1740s
Norfolk farmers begin to publicize their four-stage crop rotation, using turnips and clover, without leaving land fallow.

1776
Publication of Adam Smith's *The Wealth of Nations.*

1750–1800
Most parliamentary enclosure takes place in Britain.

1785
Robert Ransome patents the first cast-iron plowshare in Britain.

1809
François Appert of France discovers how to can food.

1811
Elkanah Watson organizes the first popular agricultural fair in the United States.

1834
Cyrus McCormick patents a horse-drawn reaper in the United States.

1837
John Deere patents a steel plow able to cut through the prairie sod.

1830
First public railway line opens in Britain.

1846
Parliament abolishes Corn Laws in the name of free trade.

1825
Erie Canal connects major waterways in the United States.

1846–51
Irish potato famine.

| 1810 | 1820 | 1830 | 1840 | 1850 | 1860 | 1880 |

1830–31
"Captain Swing" riots in Britain protest low pay and little work on farms.

1823
New Poor Law in Britain lands many rural poor in workhouses.

1814
Jethro Wood creates an American cast-iron plow.

1861
Serfdom is abolished in Russia.

1812
John Common invents a mechanical reaper in Britain.

1865
Slavery ends in the United States.

"Sowing Modernity"

The word "revolution" usually brings to mind political violence, a government toppled or a popular uprising. At its root, though, the word means a complete change—something that sets the old order of things on its ear, and brings in the new. This radical kind of change happened on farms between 1700 and 1850—first in Holland and England, ultimately throughout Europe and America. Those farms began to produce more food—more food than had ever been produced in history. The new bounty allowed the population to grow and move. It permitted workers to leave the farm for manufacturing jobs and city life. It involved changes in landownership and trade that sparked a new kind of economic and personal independence. The agricultural revolution is one of the essential changes that led people from ancient ways of living to modern ones. As historian Peter D. McClelland puts it, the first farmers using the new methods were "sowing modernity."[1]

HOW AGRICULTURE BEGAN

Certainly, agriculture was not new in 1700. Agriculture means growing domesticated plants and animals, ones that have been specially selected and bred for food. One kind of revolution occurred about eleven thousand years ago when human beings first began to practice agriculture. Most people then lived in small, mobile bands. They hunted and gathered wild plants for food. Over time, some groups discovered that it was possible to help plants grow in the wild by tending and watering them. It was a small step to selecting the best plants, moving them to protected spots, and replanting their seeds. Similarly, certain animals could be herded or kept in fenced areas. When the best of these were allowed to mate, their offspring made good eating.

The development of agriculture brought people more than food: the fibers, skins, and other products of plants and animals were useful for making clothing, containers, and many other items. Domesticated animals including horses, cattle, and camels were used for transportation and in heavy work like building.

Agriculture began independently in at least five places around the world, beginning about 8500 B.C.: Southwest Asia (the "Fertile Crescent"), China, Mesoamerica (central and southern Mexico), the Andes of South America, and the eastern United States. However, most ancient people learned about farming from neighbors, as the practice gradually spread around the world. On the linked continents of Europe and Asia, the spread was particularly rapid because similar temperate climates existed at the same latitudes across that huge landmass.

The agriculture of Southwest Asia, which began in the Fertile Crescent between the Tigris and Euphrates rivers, supplied most of the crops and domesticated animals that spread across Europe. The eight "founder crops" developed there include two kinds of wheat and one kind of barley; the pulses (beans or beanlike plants)—peas, lentils, chickpeas, and bitter vetch; and the fiber crop flax, used to make linen cloth. Wheat and barley are kinds of grains, also called cereals or (in Britain) corn. (Note that the American term for the corn that comes from a cob remains the old British term, "corn," while in Britain and the rest of Europe today, it is called by its American Indian name, "maize.")

Cereals grow quickly compared with many other plants. They produce heavy yields of food dense in calories, which give

The initial agricultural revolution occurred eleven thousand years ago when humans began to selectively breed plants (like these grapevines) and animals.

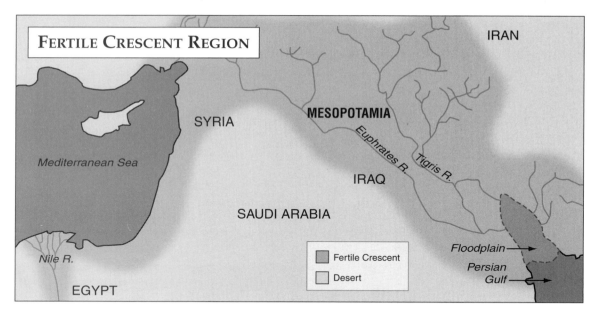

FERTILE CRESCENT REGION

IRAN

SYRIA

MESOPOTAMIA

Mediterranean Sea

Euphrates R.

Tigris R.

IRAQ

SAUDI ARABIA

Nile R.

Floodplain

Persian
Gulf

Fertile Crescent

Desert

EGYPT

people energy. About half the calories consumed in the world today come from cereals. People have other dietary needs, too, including protein. The incomplete proteins in cereals can be supplemented by pulses to form a complete diet, allowing people to live longer, healthier lives.

PLANTS AND ANIMALS BENEFIT EACH OTHER

In addition to this winning combination of plants, farmers of the Fertile Crescent domesticated four large mammals: the goat, the sheep, the pig, and the cow. Along with the horse, domesticated later in the Ukraine, these became (and remain) the most important domesticated animals. Mammals were particularly valuable for food as they could be milked, thus offering many more calories and protein than could be gained from meat alone.

The domestication of animals also benefited plants on the earliest farms: Ancient farmers soon learned that animal manure is an ideal natural fertilizer. It also allowed humans to harness animals for labor, especially in pulling plows and carts. The earliest animal-drawn plows seem to have appeared in the Fertile Crescent and Egypt about 3000 B.C. Science historian Jared Diamond explains how the plow not only made planting easier, but also allowed people to extend their cropland:

> The first prehistoric farmers of central Europe, the so-called Linearbrandkeramik culture that arose slightly before 5000 B.C., were initially confined to soils light enough to be tilled by means of hand-held digging sticks. Only over a thousand years later, with the introduction of the ox-drawn plow, were those farmers able to extend cultivation to a much wider range of heavy soils and tough sods. Similarly, Native American farmers of the North

American Great Plains grew crops in river valleys, but farming of the tough sods on the extensive uplands had to await 19th-century Europeans and their animal-drawn plows.[2]

As Diamond suggests, the extension of agriculture did not end in prehistoric times but instead has flown ahead in spurts with the introduction of new ideas and technologies. The agricultural revolution of the eighteenth and nineteenth centuries was the first big growth spurt for agriculture, after the settlement and civilization of Europe. The reasons for that lie in the way European society developed.

AGRICULTURE LEADS TO CIVILIZATION

Agriculture is sometimes said to lead to civilization, because agriculture allowed people to stay in one place instead of roaming the land. Farmers must stay near their crops to plant, tend, and harvest them. And agricultural harvests were intended to be large enough to last through the year, or at least through the winter. That means a need for storage of grains and beans and roots. Moving with such a surplus becomes difficult or impossible.

A settled society with a surplus of food needed to protect that surplus. Strong leaders supported by armies developed for that purpose. Leaders also determined how the surplus was to be divided. Social ranks developed that supported the leadership, and reflected the division of wealth. Civilization flowered as those with surplus wealth sup-

ported specialists such as scribes, artists, builders, and planners, who enriched the way of life. Trade among groups developed, some of it long-distance, though many local areas remained isolated.

By 1600, European civilization had a long and complex history, and its achievements were uncountable. Yet on the farm, in most places, little had changed in agricultural methods since the ox-drawn plow first appeared in central Europe in 5000 B.C. The social and political pattern of strong leadership and social divisions was generally

Ancient farmers, such as these Egyptians, brought in harvests that supported their complex civilization.

conservative. Bad weather or disease often wiped out crops, and leaders tried to leave as little to chance as possible. Experiments were frowned upon. In addition, patterns of belief placed the welfare of the harvest not in the hands of the farmer but in the hands of God. Religious leaders blessed the planting and welcomed the harvest with festivals.

Population growth was limited by the amount of food produced. However, though famine could lead to starvation, more often low food supplies led to reduced population by more indirect means. When the number of people and demand for food exceeded the amount of food available, food prices would rise, making the cost of living higher. Families could only afford less food of poorer quality. Illness would increase as a result, and more disease caused more deaths, especially of the very old and very young. The problem was made worse by a lack of ways to send surplus food from better-producing areas to areas of famine. As population fell, so did demand for food. Low demand meant food prices fell, which gave farmers little incentive to produce more.

The agricultural revolution promised to end this pattern. Population statistics are hard to come by for very early times, but in Britain, for example, beginning in the 1200s, the population seemed to have a top limit of 5 to 6 million people. When the population reached this maximum in the early 1300s, and again in the mid-1600s, it stopped growing. Yet in the mid-1700s, the population passed the 6 million mark without hesitation. By 1830 over 12 million people were living in Britain. As production increased, food prices remained affordable. And instead of 75 to 80 percent of the people working on farms, only 20 percent were working there by 1850. Fewer people were producing two-and-a-half to three times as much farm produce in 1850 as they were when this remarkable revolution began around 1700. In the span of 150 years, new ideas, inventions, and technologies took root in the churned-up soil of changing social and economic institutions. The amazing transformation that resulted was a turning point in world history.

Chapter

1 Traditional Farming in Europe

At the dawn of the agricultural revolution, in the 1600s, Europeans were farming much as they had farmed for hundreds of years. Old patterns of landownership and traditional farming methods, most dating from the Middle Ages, produced about the same amount of food year after year. When weather or war took a toll on the crops, or the population grew, shortages were the result and famine threatened.

THE LEGACY OF FEUDALISM

All over Europe, land for crops and grazing remained largely under the control of a relatively small number of people. Under the medieval feudal system, all land in a country technically belonged to a king. He allowed his lords or knights to "hold" pieces of land in return for their loyalty and service. In turn, the lords allowed farmers to hold land in return for their services, generally part of their crops and livestock. The word "farmer" comes from an old French word meaning "tenant," one who pays rent for use of land.

By the 1600s, many large estates, known as manors, remained in the hands of wealthy owners—often the descendants of feudal

lords and knights. These wealthy people also generally made up the ruling class of each nation. Their lands were worked by farmers under a wide variety of agreements or tenancies. In some parts of Europe, including England, France, and the Low Countries (today's Netherlands and Belgium), the medieval system had faded, but not disappeared. While large individual manors remained, some independent small farmers held their own land, often paying a token fee to the local lord for that right. The term "peasant" is sometimes used for these small independent farmers, but it is also used to mean tenant farmers or resident workers on large estates. Historian Robert Zaller helps explain how feudalism was changing, especially for peasants in France:

> Feudalism did not simply vanish; it was gradually modified into something else. . . . Over the centuries, the peasant had acquired most of the rights we associate with ownership— the right to sell, lease, exchange, give, and bequeath—while technically his land still remained part of a feudal proprietorship. In practice this meant that his exercise of these rights was still subject to the approval of the lord. No

Under the medieval feudal system, European peasants were required to give part of their harvest to wealthy lords who owned or controlled the land.

property could be transferred without the lord's consent and without payment of dues that often robbed the peasant of his profit. The lord was also entitled to substitute himself as purchaser at the same price.[3]

In parts of Europe, serfs remained under medieval laws and conditions long after the Renaissance of 1400–1550. These people farmed under the complete control of their lord and were not allowed to leave the lord's land. The lord held a lifelong right to their labor. The serf system existed in eastern Europe and Denmark well into the 1700s, and in Russia until 1861.

Nearly everyone belonged to the farming economy. Peasant families made up 80 percent of the population of France around 1700, for example. About nine of every ten Russians was a serf or a peasant. Even in England, where changes on the land were beginning to happen in the 1600s, about 75 percent of the working population was employed on the land.

Laws of inheritance made a great difference in the form farms took across Europe. In Britain the rule of primogeniture meant that the first son would generally inherit the parents' property, whether it was a cottage and garden or a large estate. This meant that farms could remain large enough to work profitably. In some areas, such as Ireland and northern Spain, the custom of dividing land among several children led to tiny plots that barely produced enough to keep the owners alive. In Britain parents did attempt to find other work or compensation for sons who were not to inherit. (It was assumed that girls would marry.) Records show, for instance, that a Durham farmer with two sons was advised "to put one of his said children to be prentice [apprenticed] to some good occupation, whereby he might be able to earn his leavings in tyme to come, and thereby he mighte be more liberall to that childe which he meant to traine and bring up in husbandrie [farming]."[4]

The way of life of the farm families varied depending on the location and nature of the farm. In Russia and eastern Europe, serfs living in villages on the largest estates were expected to deliver a large part of their farm produce to their lord. The richest Russian

A Day's Work

Gervase Markham, in his work Farewell to Husbandry *(1623), laid out what a farmer should be doing every hour of a late winter day. His instruction is reprinted on* Wayne Rasmussen's Readings in the History of American Agriculture.

Wee will suppose it to bee after Christmas, and about plow day (which is the first letting out of the plow) . . . the Plowman shall rise before foure of the clocke in the morning, and after thanks given to God for his rest, and the successe of his labors, he shall goe into his stable, or beast house, and first he shall fodder his cattle, then cleanse the house, and make the boothes cleane; rubbe downe the cattle, and cleanse their skinnes from all filth, then hee shall curry his horses, rubbe them with cloathes and wispes [of hay] . . . and then hee shall water both his oxen and horses, and housing them againe, give them more fodder, and to his horse by all means provender, as chaffe and dry Pease and Beanes. . . .

And whilst they are eating their meat [food], he shal make readie his collars, humes, treates, halters, mullens, and plowgeares [harness materials], seeing everything fit, and in his due place, and to these labours I will also allow full two houres, that is, from foure of the clocke, till six, then shall he come in to breakfast . . . so that at seven of the clocke he may set forward to his labour, and then hee shall plow from seven of the clocke till two or three in the afternoone, then he shall unyoake and bring home his cattel, and having rubb'd them; drest them, and cleansed away all durt and filth, he shall fodder them, and give them meat, then shall the servants goe in to their dinner . . . it will then bee towards foure of the clocke, at which time hee shall goe to his cattle againe, and rubbing them downe, and cleansing their stalls, give them more fodder . . . and by this time it will draw past six of the clocke, at what time he shall come in to supper; and after supper hee shall either by the fire side, mend shooes both for himself and their family, or beat and knocke hempe, or flaxe, or picke and stampe apples, or crabs [crabapples] for cider . . . or else grinde malt on the quernes [mortar and pestle], picke candle-rushes, or doe some husbandly [farm-related] office within doores till it be full eight a clocke: Then shall he take his Lanthorne and candle, and goe to his cattle; and having cleansed the stalles and plankes, litter them downe, looke that they be safely tyed, and then fodder and give them meat for all night, then giving God thankes for benefits received that day, let him and the whole household goe to their rest till the next morning.

lords owned enough serfs to fill cities: one lord, Peter Seremetev, gained 140,000 serfs through his marriage and inheritance. Over the course of his life another 45,600 serfs were added to his rolls. Russian landlords thought of serfs as wealth, but they needed so many partly because the serfs themselves were not often eager workers. A common saying of the time in Russia was, "Better become poor by sleeping than by working."[5] Why work hard when the lord took all the reward?

A Russian serf family meets with their lord. The relationship between the Russian serf and his lord was one of strict bondage.

RENTS AND TAXES AND TITHES

Farmers who rented land, or held small farms of their own, had at least some expectation of gain from their own work. However, rents and taxes could be, and often were, so heavy that simply keeping the farm going was all people could manage. It was a fact that the land remained almost the only source of wealth, and it had to pay for the government, the church, armies, and aristocrats, who in turn could pay skilled workers such as accountants and jewelers. Many trades, from weaving to milling, were done by people who lived on farms and did some farmwork, too.

In medieval times, rents and taxes were generally collected by the lord; by the 1600s, landlord, government, and church generally shared the task. But the many ways of skimming some of the wealth of the land from those who farmed it remained the same. Some of them were named in an old German royal decree:

> Every official is to report annually . . . how much profit he made with the oxen in the service of our cowherds, how much he made off the manses [lands belonging to certain houses] to provide plowing, how much from pig tax and other [property] taxes he collected, how much he has received in fines and how much for keeping the peace [court fees], how much for game caught without our permission in our forests, how much from fines, [fees] from mills, forests, pastures . . . how much rent from foresters and tilthing [planting] areas on cultivated lands belonging to the crown, the income

A French lord arrives on his estate to collect rent. Medieval French farmers were obligated to pay rent to the lord, tithes to the church, and taxes to the government.

from markets, vinyards, and from the wine tax.[6]

French farmers paid a particularly long list of taxes, fees, and rents. These varied from place to place, but in general, there were four kinds of taxes due to the state, and taxes called tithes due to the church. To the lord, owner of the property, the tenant farmer paid some rent in kind (crops or livestock) and some rent in cash. Even if the farmer owned his own acres, he had to pay the lord on transfer of property. He had to

put in time repairing roads, or else pay another fee, and had to pay for use of the local lord's mill, winepress, and bakery (no others were allowed). Rents and taxes were an important limitation on incomes from farming.

THE COMMON FIELDS SYSTEM

Landholding determined what was produced and who gained from it. Yet that was only part of the story. Regardless of the owner or the tenant, there were traditional ways of using the land that helped determine production and profit. One of the most important was the common fields system. Some farmers had houses on the fields they worked. But many more Europeans of the 1600s lived in fairly compact villages and worked the land around the village. On large estates such as those in Russia or southern Spain, the villagers cooperated to farm the lord's lands. In other countries such as England, France, and northern Italy, land around the village might be owned or rented in a variety of ways by the villagers. Yet everyone held common rights to certain uses of the land. Forested areas, for instance, might technically belong to the lord, but villagers might keep the right to hunt, to gather firewood, and to release pigs in the forest to forage for nuts. Pasture was often considered "commons," where all villagers could allow their animals to graze.

Villagers also often cooperated in working their fields. In England, for instance, it was normal for each family to have a small garden next to the home for growing vegetables and whatever the family wished. The family's main farm fields, however, were a variety of strips of land scattered around the village. Villagers often plowed all the fields cooperatively, and they harvested in the same way. Village farmers followed certain common rules that regulated times and methods of farming and gave each villager his or her due. The rules were set by the overseer of the manor, or where a manor held less power, by a village meeting. Arrangements in the village of Cheddar, for instance, where the famous cheese was first made, were described by a visitor in the early 1700s. On a large common pasture, he wrote:

> The whole herd of the cows, belonging to the town, do feed; the ground is exceedingly rich, and as the whole village are cowkeepers, they take care to keep up the goodness of the soil, by agreeing to lay on large quantities of dung for manuring, and enriching the land.
>
> The milk of all the town cows is brought together every day into a common room, where the persons appointed, or trusted, for the management, measure every man's quantity, and set it down in a book; when the quantities are adjusted, the milk is all put together, and every meal's milk makes one cheese, and no more; so that the cheese is bigger, or less, as the cows yield more, or less milk. By this method, the goodness of the cheese is preserved . . . .
>
> As the cheeses are, by this means, very large, for they often weigh a hundred weight . . . so the poorer inhabitants, who have but few cows, are obliged to stay [wait] the longer for the return of their milk [the payment for their milk], for no man has such return, till his share comes to a whole cheese . . . and thus every man has equal justice.[7]

TASKS ON THE FARM

The major tasks of farming—plowing, fertilizing, planting, hoeing, harvesting, feeding animals, milking, egg gathering, slaughtering—are the basic tasks required to produce food to the present day. However, the tools and methods used in the 1600s were much the same as those used centuries before. Plowing was the first task of the year, necessary to break up the heavy earth and provide air spaces into which seeds could fall. Heavy wooden plows were pulled by oxen, which are neutered bulls of a sturdy species of cattle. It took several people to manage the slow-witted animals and get the plow to move in a straight line. The word "acre" originally meant the amount of land that could be plowed in a day. It is not a large area.

In their fields, European farmers grew grain, generally wheat, rye, oats, or barley. The grain, all of it called "corn" by the British, provided bread, the staff of life, and was the basis for ale. Seeds were planted by the "broadcast" method. A person walked up and down the plowed field with a sack or a

BREAKING COMMONS RULES

Records for the English village of Foxton show the kinds of rules most common fields villages had—and what happened when they were broken. These were collected by Rowland Parker in a history of his village, The Common Stream: Portrait of an English Village Through 2,000 Years.

John Hille, servant and shepherd of John Thirlowe, and Henry Sadeler, servant and shepherd of Richard Newman, with their flocks of sheep trespassed in the fields and stubbles and other growing pasture, contrary to the bye-laws; so they are fined 40d [40 pence].

John Everard, butcher, overloaded the commons and pastures of this village with his oxen and cattle, to the detriment of all tenants and residents; fined 10s [10 shillings].

All tenants and residents of this village shall ring their pigs and piglets every year from Michaelmas to Christmas so that they do not grub up the soil or several pastures; on pain of 40d for every offence, 20d to the Lady of the Manor, 20d to the upkeep of the church.

No one shall carry away the common dung made in the street unless for every two cart-loads of dung he shall carry back one load of stones into the roads of Foxton.

John Everard, butcher, allowed his dunghill to drain into the common stream of this village, to the serious detriment of the tenants and residents; fined 4d; pain of 10s.

Ordered that ducks, geese, and pigs shall not frequent the common brook running in the middle of the village, but shall either sell them or keep them within their tenements or houses; pain of 3s.4d.

basket of seed, casting it out by the handful. Some seed fell in spots where it could not grow, and the planting was uneven. Once seed was sown, it was harrowed: a heavy wood frame with teeth on the bottom was pulled across the field, possibly by an ox, but often by a man. The harrow further pulverized the soil and pulled it over the seeds to assure that they were well under the ground. The work of sowing barley (a grain used mostly for brewing beer) is described in an old rhyming agricultural calendar by Thomas Tusser. His rhymes were first printed in 1557, but were used to teach schoolchildren as late as the 1800s:

> Sow barley in March, in April, and May,
> the later in sand, the sooner in clay.
> What worser for barley, than wetness and cold?
> what better to skillfull, than time to be bold?

> Who soweth his barley too soon, or in rain,
> of oats and of thistles shall after complain:
> I speak not of May-weed, of Cockle and such,
> that noieth [bothers] the barley, so often and much.

> Let barley be harrowed, finely as dust,
> then workmanly trench it, and fence it ye must.
> This season well plied, set sowing an end,
> and praise and pray God, a good harvest to send.[8]

A "trench," or ditch, might be for drainage, or for irrigation. Many old fields were created with wide ridges alternating with trenches. Wooden fences had to be built to keep wild animals and also grazing animals

A medieval farmer casts handfuls of seed onto a plowed field. In the background, a harrow driven by oxen pulls soil over the seeds.

THE RIDDLE OF THE FLAIL'S SWEPLE

The flail is a tool used for threshing grain and features a wood handle attached by chain to a shorter wood rod called a sweple. The worker struck the pile of grain on the barn floor with the sweple so that the bouncing and vibrating loosened the grain itself from the "ear" on which it grew. Harvesters enjoyed this riddle, translated by Dorothy Hartley in her book Lost Country Life. *It was first printed in the* Exeter Book of Riddles, *probably eighth century in origin. It begins, "Fettered with rings," meaning "tied with chain."*

Fettered with rings, I work intermittently
Obeying my ruler, who is also my server.
When I break into my bed, is made known by the rattle
Of the chains round my neck, set on me, by my Maker.
Often mankind, sometimes a woman, comes to awake me
When I'm heavy with sleep, in the cold of the winter.
With hot-hearted anger they rouse me, till one, hot and fiercely
Breaks the rings bound upon me—
Which pleases my ruler, my server, who then standeth idle,
He's a poor foolish fellow, who can do nothing without me.
Who am I? The sweple of a flail.

off the crop. Weeds were an eternal problem: the "May-weed" and "Cockle" were going to trouble the crop of the best farmer. Men, women, and children spent time hoeing by hand in the fields while grain was growing.

HARVEST WORK FOR ALL HANDS

The hard work of plowing, sowing, and weeding was nothing compared with harvesting. Bringing in the grain took the effort of every soul in the village. Wheat and rye were reaped with the sickle, a curved knife that was used to saw off an armful of grain. Both men and women used the sickle. Another tool, the scythe, was generally used for mowing oats and barley. The scythe had a long wooden handle attached at a right angle to a blade about two feet long. It was generally used with a swinging motion as the farmer stood upright, and was too heavy for most women to wield. Behind the harvest cutters came teams who raked the grain, tied it into sheaves, and then set it in stooks, or piles with peaked tops, to dry. Next the grain was taken to the barn or set into large piles called ricks, which were thatched on top to keep out rain.

The harvest complete, all villagers (in practice, mostly women and children) were allowed onto the fields to glean: to pick up any remaining grain for their own use. The basis of gleaning lay in Moses's pronouncement in the Bible: "And when ye reap the harvest of your land, thou shalt not wholly reap the corners of thy field, nor shalt thou gather gleanings of the harvest . . . thou shalt leave them for the poor and stranger."[9] Manor and village laws regulated gleaning, but it was practiced everywhere, and could net a good gleaner up to a fifth of a year's livelihood.

To process the grain, workers first cut the grain heads or ears from the stalks, saving the stalks for animal feed. Then the grain itself had to be separated from its outer covering, a process called threshing. Threshers beat the grain with flails, long wooden handles with shorter free-swinging sticks on their ends. Next they winnowed the grain, tossing it in the air to let the wind take away the light outer parts. Then it was ready to store in sacks, to be used or milled as needed.

Threshing could continue in the barn well into the winter because it took so long to accomplish. People were used to long days of work, ruled by the rising and setting of the sun. Though the work was hard, part of the rhythm of rural life were the many holidays: twenty-seven in England in the 1600s (down from fifty a hundred years earlier), not counting Sundays. Most of these were religious holidays such as saints' days, but some were connected directly to farming. On Plough Monday, the plough was paraded through the village. At Rogationtide, everyone marched around the boundaries of the farmlands to reaffirm their legal edges. The holidays helped bind the villagers and the lord of the manor and the church together in tradition and belief. No one thought they were a waste of valuable time.

WOMEN REAP "AS WELL AS YOU"

Women were essential to farm life, doing a thousand necessary jobs in the household and garden. They were often in charge of the dairy. Women carried extra produce to market, and did the buying and the selling there. Heavy outdoor work, especially at harvest time, was also part of their lives, as described in this rhyme by Mary Collier (1739):

> When Harvest comes, into the Field we go,
> And help to reap the Wheat as well as you,
> Or else we go the ears of Corn to glean,
> No Labour scorning, be it e'er so mean,
> But in the Work we freely bear a part,
> And what we can, perform with all our Heart.[10]

After 1750 in Britain, the number of things women did on farms generally declined, and tasks were more strictly divided on the farm between men's work and women's work. That helps explain why a visitor was so surprised when he looked in on some old-fashioned Devonshire farms, untouched by the "improvements" of the 1700s:

> Farmers of every class (some few excepted) carry their corn into the field, on horseback, perhaps a quarter of a mile, from the barn, to the summit of some airy swell; where it is winnowed, *by women!* the mistress of the farm, perhaps, being exposed in the severest weather, to the cutting winds of winter. . . . The [past] practice of the Northern extremity of the Island, in which farmers loaded their wives and daughters with dung,

to be carried to the fields on their backs, was but a little more civilized. [11]

ANIMALS AND SOIL RENEWAL

The raising of animals was as much a part of farming as cropping. Cattle, pigs, goats, sheep, and chickens were the most important farm animals, as they still are today. These animals were the source not only of meat, eggs, and milk but also of hides, tallow (fat) for candles and soap, horn and hoofs, feathers, and wool. Some farmers, such as the Cheddar villagers, kept only animals, moving them as needed to follow advantageous climate or food sources. Enormous flocks of sheep in Spain were herded many miles according to the seasons, a ritual called the Mesta. Similarly, Alpine farmers sent their goats to high mountain meadows to graze on summer grasses. It was most common, however, for farmers to raise both animals and crops, because each benefited the other. The animals ate hay and other fodder grown on the farm; some could even eat the weeds that grew up on land that was worn out from growing crops. And the animal manure that enriched the soil was vital to crops.

Two women milk cows while a third pours the milk into a churn at a dairy farm. Throughout history, women have performed a variety of farm jobs.

Once crops have been grown in one spot for a time, the soil loses its fertility, making harvests smaller and smaller. Farmers have known this since ancient times, though they did not know that the scientific reason for it is loss of nitrogen in the soil. Nitrogen can be replaced in a variety of ways. One way is fallowing: leaving land unplanted for a year or more, to "rest" before it is planted again. Fallowing was practiced all over Europe, making a certain amount of land unprofitable each year. In Britain, many farmers used the "three-field" system. They planted one grain crop on a field, followed it the next year with a different grain crop, then fallowed the field the third year. This meant that about a third of the farmland was unproductive in any given year.

A second way to replenish the nutrients of the soil is to fertilize it. In some parts of Europe, seaweed, chalky earth, and other materials were used as fertilizers. Waste from towns was also spread on fields. But by far the most useful and common fertilizer was animal dung. Farmers commonly moved animals from pasture land during the day to fallow land at night, so they could deposit dung there and make it more fertile. Sheep were especially valued for this purpose because they manured evenly and tramped the dung into the earth with their feet. In winter, animal stalls were shoveled out into the dung cart, and then the dung was shoveled onto the fields—even if they were frozen and covered with snow. An old English rhyme for February included the verse, "Land-meadow that yearly is spread for hay, now fence it and spare it and dung it ye may."[12]

In village-centered common fields systems, all the animals of the village were generally managed together (as was the case in the town of Cheddar). The custom was helpful in saving labor for the villagers, but it also limited the amount of change any one farmer could make. If the sheep were moved onto the harvest stubble at a certain time, any unusual strips—requiring different harvest times—might not get the valuable manure. And any farmer hoping to mate his animals carefully to gain improved young could not do it if his animals were always with the others. They would find partners among any of the other animals, and their breeding could not be controlled.

DIVIDING FARM PRODUCTS

Any farmer, from serf to independent landholder, had first to support his own family. In the 1600s, most farmers were nearly self-sufficient, growing or making whatever they needed at home. The most self-sufficient farmers raised all they needed except salt: an important reason for the heavy salt tax in France. This and other taxes and rents took part of the produce of the farm to pay for the government, the church, and the landlord class. Other produce beyond what the farmer needed to live went to market.

In general, markets were the chief means by which food and other farm goods were spread among those who did not benefit from the rents and taxes. There were few shops in the Europe of the 1600s. Instead, farmers took excess produce to open markets on certain market days. Fairs, held more rarely, allowed for the regional or specialized sale of certain animals or other goods.

Open markets were the main sources of food for Europeans who did not own or work farm land. Before the agricultural revolution, local market rules often restricted trade.

Rules set by local lords or officials governed what happened at the market. In England, the rules generally limited profits for farmers and for reseller middlemen in favor of making sure nonfarmers could buy food cheaply. These were the rules for one Wiltshire market, set in 1564:

1. Before the market starts the sellers of grain are to agree with the local justices what the price should be.

2. No transactions may take place before 9 A.M. when a bell will be tolled 20 times.
3. When the market opens purchases must be for the customer's own use and be limited to 2 bushels of grain.
4. After 11 A.M. (when the bell is again tolled 20 times) grain may be bought by those who will resell it (e.g. bakers, brewers, and badgers [middlemen]).

5. Those buying grain to resell must be licensed by a Justice of the Peace.
6. Grain may only be bought on market day.
7. No person may buy grain in the market if she has sufficient of her own. [13]

Such rules restricted the profits of farmers and discouraged the free exchange of goods. However, some trade certainly was possible, including long-distance trade. English wool, for instance, found good markets around the world from the time of Queen Elizabeth I (who reigned from 1558 to 1603). Grain from the serf-farmed estates of Russia and eastern Europe was exported to fill needs elsewhere in Europe when harvests failed. Yet for most peasants and small farmers, trade did not promise much benefit. Besides the market restrictions, it was slow and expensive to move products over the poor roads. In 1700 the price of English coal doubled as soon as it was transported five miles. It is not surprising, then, that statistics show that when English farmers of this period produced more than they needed, they generally worked less as their reward, instead of spending their profit on new goods or farm improvements.

In the 1600s, though, there were pockets of change in farms and markets. A real hotbed for these changes was in Holland, where Dutch farmers were already exporting their ideas to a few progressive farmers in England.

Chapter

2 New Crops and New Methods

Change came to traditional European farming from many different directions as the 1600s came to an end. One innovation built upon another so that a momentum for change developed. By the 1750s, farmers were producing much more food than Europe had ever seen before, and the population began to grow with unprecedented speed.

NEW CROPS FROM THE AMERICAS

One source of change came originally from far across the sea: a new set of plants from North and South America. These included maize (corn), potatoes, and tobacco, plus a range of vegetables including tomatoes and peppers. Many of the new plants first arrived in Europe in the 1500s, with Spain's returning explorers and conquistadores. Yet they were only very slowly accepted. Europeans worried that some of the exotic foods might be unsafe to eat. Both tomatoes and potatoes, for instance, were known to be members of the belladonna plant family, of which many members are poisonous. Other plants were slow to spread because they did not grow well in all climates and soils of Europe. Maize, for example, needed both heat and plenty of rain to grow well.

So did tomatoes, although in time, people living along the dry Mediterranean coast discovered that they could grow wonderful tomatoes as long as they watered them artificially.

Maize and potatoes were the most successful of the new food crops, largely because they produced several times more calories per acre planted than the standard European bread-making grains, wheat and rye. By the 1700s, maize was being planted regularly in the upland valleys of Italy, Greece, and areas just to their north. The maize was not so much a sellable crop as a means of subsistence for poor farmers. Dried ground corn was made into a mush, called polenta in Italy, which fed hungry families when there was nothing else to eat. Potatoes grew well in cooler climates, and also fed the poor. Unlike grains, potatoes did not store well for a very long time, and so it was difficult to sell them on a large scale. Besides, potatoes were thought of at first as an animal food, or fodder, not elegant enough to grace a fine dining table. For peasants, however, potatoes could be a lifeline.

The nutritional value of a potato is remarkable. Potatoes can supply nearly every daily food need, including protein, starch, and vitamins, to keep people healthy (unlike

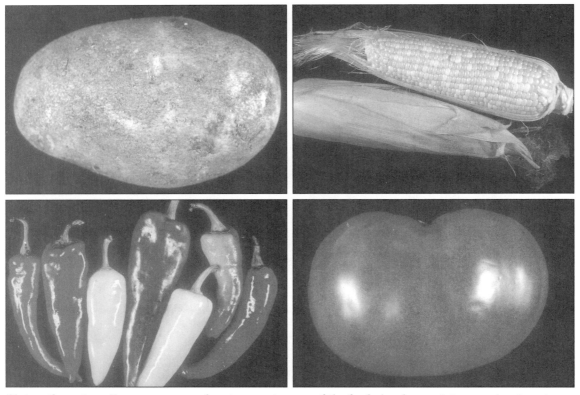

Sixteenth-century Europeans were slow to accept many of the foods (such as potatoes, maize, tomatoes, and peppers) Spanish explorers brought from the New World.

corn, which must be supplemented to avoid the niacin-deficiency disease pellagra, which caused great suffering in Italy). Furthermore, enough potatoes can be grown on a tiny amount of land to feed a large family—and its animals. It is likely that Spanish sailors first brought this valuable food to Ireland, the first country in Europe to make good use of the spud. In the mid-1600s the English took over Ireland and banished most native Irish to the far west. The impoverished Irish, living either in the rainy, crowded west, or working on English-owned farms, learned to depend on the potato because they could not grow or buy wheat for bread. In 1780 an English visitor to Ireland gave this description, looking down his nose at the habits of the poor:

> Mark the Irishman's potato bowl placed on the floor, the whole family upon their hams [squatting] around it, devouring a quantity almost incredible, the beggar seating himself to it with a welcome, the pig taking his share as readily as the wife, the cock, hens, turkeys, geese, the cur [dog], the cat, and perhaps the cow—all partaking of the same dish. No man can often have been a witness of it without being convinced of the plenty, and I will add, the cheerfulness that attends it. [14]

Potatoes were slower to arrive in northern Europe. They first gained a foothold as animal fodder, which could be grown on the fallow fields being readied for rye. Because they were a new crop, they remained tax free in many places. And because they could be left in the ground most of the winter, and only dug up to be eaten as needed, marauding armies could not take them as they did bags of grain. By the 1740s some rulers were deciding that potatoes were a good, cheap way to keep their workers alive. King William of Germany and King Frederick the Great of Prussia began campaigns to introduce potatoes as a food to their people. A few wagonloads of potatoes rotted as the peasants stared at them suspiciously. But they soon caught on with the help of laws. One law called for a peasant's ears and nose to be cut off if he refused to plant and eat potatoes.

By 1800, potatoes were essential to the diet of farming and working people all across northern Europe—even, finally, in England. Historians Herman J. Viola and Carolyn Margolis have summed up the impact of American corn and potatoes on Europeans this way:

> Taking Europe as a whole, it seems clear that American food crops were an essential resource for the nineteenth-century surge of numbers, wealth, and power that raised European nations so

The nutrient-rich potato gradually established itself as a staple in the diets of farmers and workers across northern Europe.

far above the rest of the world. The labor force that sustained Europe's intensified urban activities—industrial, commercial, administrative—could not have been fed without them. The flood of emigrants who peopled the Americas and other lands overseas could not have survived infancy without the extra calories that came from potatoes and maize.[15]

TURNIPS, CLOVER, AND NEWS FROM NORFOLK

As the new crops from the Americas were gaining ground, some old European crops were being revived for new purposes. A literal seedbed for agricultural ideas existed in the Low Countries: Holland, Brabant, and Flanders (today's Netherlands and Belgium). Populations in these countries were tiny, and the first large population to benefit from most of their ideas was British. Farmers in Britain took the Low Countries' ideas and ran with them, expanding and building on them in novel ways. That is why Britain is generally viewed as the birthplace of the agricultural revolution.

In the Low Countries, relatively wealthy farmers had only very limited land to cultivate. They looked for ways to gain the maximum from a little space. One way was the development of field turnips (a variation on the well-known garden turnips). Turnip tops gave animals better nutrition than grass into early winter, and the turnips themselves made good fodder through the late winter and spring. During the late 1600s and early 1700s, turnip growing spread in England. A farm steward in Lincolnshire wrote in 1728,

"Now of late, since the practice of improveing lands with turnops is set up, [estate owners] either take that way of so improveing their own lands and feeding the sheep themselves, or sell 'em (tho leane) into those countrys where they do practice the turnop improvement."[16] Later in the century, frost-resistant Swedish turnips ("swedes") and other roots such as mangels joined the English list.

At about the same time as the "turnop improvement," improved clovers also spread from Holland to England. Clover, like other deliberately planted pasture plants including alfalfa and sainfoin, gave animals better nutrition than ordinary grass. In addition, clover, like others in the legume plant family, actually added fertility to the soil. While grain crops like wheat and barley rob the soil of nitrogen, clover helps to fix nitrogen in the soil. Certainly, farmers were unaware of how the fertility improved, but they realized that clover was beneficial. An English writer of the time noted, "After the three or four first years of Clovering, it will so frame the earth, that it will be very fit to Corn [grain] again, which will be a very great advantage."[17] Clover played a role in the practice of convertible husbandry, which spread over the 1600s. This meant alternating arable (crop) land and pasture land over a long period of years.

Turnips, clover, convertible husbandry, and other ideas that had long been stewing in England and the Low Countries came together very forcefully in the county of Norfolk, England, in the 1740s. That is the time when documents show that three farms were among the first to use what became known as the "Norfolk system," one of the major breakthroughs of the agricultural

IMPROVEMENT IN A SCOTTISH VILLAGE

In the 1790s Reverend William Blackie recorded the state of agriculture in Yetholm, Scotland. He mentions the key crop of turnips and an effort to improve the sheep breed—signs that improvement was coming to Yetholm. About fifty years later, Reverend John Baird in the same place reported more cropland in use, plus regular four- or five-shift crop rotations and new breeds of sheep, showing that the village was taking full advantage of the new ideas of the agricultural revolution. Their accounts appear in the article "History of Industry and Employment in the Parish" in modern-day Yetholm's Web site.

Rev. William Blackie:

About 1170 English acres are actually under tillage, and though there be some wheat sown, yet the greatest part is laid out in raising barley and oats, and turnips. Even the small tenants, who have from 1 and 2 to 10 and 15 acres . . . have their turnip quarter, for which, on account of their vicinity to Northumberland, they find a ready market, getting, when a good crop, some years 3 pounds and others 5 pounds, to be eaten upon the ground with sheep. Much more land could be made arable.

The sheep maintained in summer are about 4800. They are generally the largest of the Cheviot breed. . . . A good many years ago, a trial was made in a neighboring parish, farther up the Bowmont water, of crossing with the Bakewell breed; but it was found far from being an improvement, and they sold them off as speedily as possible.

Rev. John Baird:

There are more than 6000 acres in the parish, of which more than 2600 are arable [cropland]. . . .

The mode of cultivation adopted in this parish is usually what is called the four- and five-shift rotation, the former being practiced in the village lands, the latter on the larger farms. This mode of husbandry consists of taking a crop of turnips the first year; a crop of wheat or barley, sown with grass, the second year; a crop of hay the third year; and a crop of oats the fourth year. According to the five-shift rotation, the ground is allowed to lie in pasture the fourth year, and on the fifth it is ploughed up and sown with oats. One fifth nearly of the arable land of the parish is annually sown off with turnips.

The number of sheep in the parish may be about 4800; of these about 1800 may be Leicester, 1000 Cheviot, and 2,000 half-bred, or a cross between the other two.

revolution. The farmers in Norfolk had some advantages: their soil was relatively light and easy to cultivate—unlike heavy clay soils elsewhere, and the farms were relatively large, but not so large that the farmers could not personally carry out detailed plans for their lands.

The Norfolk system called for planting crops in a basic four-course rotation, instead of three, and replacing the fallow period with planted clover. On any given field, the rotation went from clover to wheat, wheat to roots (swedes or turnips), roots to barley or oats or both, and back to clover. Individual farms varied the routine and sometimes held the land under one crop or the other more than a year. Benefits and profits were gained all along the way. Clover fattened animals, some of which could be sold, and enriched the soil for wheat. Once the wheat was sold,

manure from the animals was spread on the land and roots were grown for further fodder, creating the chance to raise even more valuable animals. Another manuring then led to the planting of barley and oats. The barley was sold, mostly for brewing beer, and the oats could be sold and also fed to the animals who contributed more manure; and then the rotation returned to clover. Norfolk farm statistics show that grain yields per acre in Norfolk remained about the same, between nine and eleven bushels, from 1250 to 1739. But in the next hundred years they doubled, to twenty-one—thanks, largely, to the Norfolk four-course system.

By 1800 the Norfolk system was well established in Norfolk and had become famous all over England. Farmers in other regions of the country imitated it entirely or in part, with profitable results.

A flock of sheep feeds on turnips. Turnips provide better nutrition to grazing animals than grass, and turnips can be grown throughout the winter.

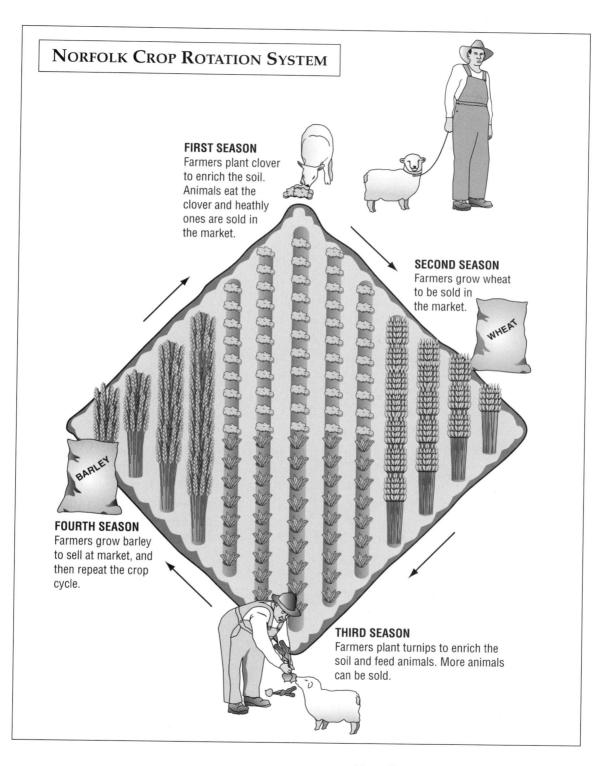

NORFOLK CROP ROTATION SYSTEM

FIRST SEASON
Farmers plant clover to enrich the soil. Animals eat the clover and heathly ones are sold in the market.

SECOND SEASON
Farmers grow wheat to be sold in the market.

WHEAT

BARLEY

FOURTH SEASON
Farmers grow barley to sell at market, and then repeat the crop cycle.

THIRD SEASON
Farmers plant turnips to enrich the soil and feed animals. More animals can be sold.

THE ROLE OF ANIMALS

It was not only greater grain yield that made the Norfolk system so successful. It also depended on, and produced, high-quality animals. Sheep, cattle, and pigs all benefited from more, and more nutritious, food available on the "improved" farms. The total number of live animals in England did not change much between 1700 and 1850. But the estimated amount of animal products, including meat, hides, wool, and tallow, actually increased by two and a half times. No one could measure the manure the well-fed animals produced, but certainly it increased, leading to greater yields from well-fertilized crops. The increase in animal products suggests that animals were growing and fattening more quickly, with new ones taking the places of slaughtered animals more often.

Changes in the breeds of animals also probably increased the amount of animal products, although that is difficult to judge since breeding of new animals had been going on for centuries in England. Certainly, new breeds were given more attention and more publicity as the 1700s came to an end. Specialty animal breeders joined ordinary farmers in creating new, more profitable breeds. One of these breeders, Robert Bakewell, developed the long wool New Leicester sheep, which benefited from turnip growing in Leicestershire. English novelist and journalist Daniel Defoe, visiting the area, noted that most of the gentlemen of the area were "grasiers," managers of sheep herds. Defoe added that a grasier not born to the aristocracy could also rise through his riches:

In some places the grasiers are so rich, that they grow [become] gentlemen. . . . The sheep bred in this county and Lincolnshire, which joins to it, are, without comparison, the largest, and bear not only the greatest weight of flesh on their bones, but also the greatest fleeces of wool on their backs of any sheep in England; nor is the fineness of the wool abated for the quantity; but as 'tis the longest staple (so the clothiers call it) so 'tis the finest wool in the whole island. . . . These are the funds of sheep which furnish the city of London, with their large mutton in so incredible a quantity.[18]

REGAINING WASTELAND

Another way in which more crops and animals were grown was through the recovery of "waste." That is the term English farmers used for land that was not pasture or arable land, for some reason. Sometimes the "waste" was too sandy or too heavy with clay. Sometimes it was marshy or stony. Farmers had always toiled to improve land, but in the eighteenth century those efforts increased as the idea took hold that land could be made to produce more than in the past.

The Low Countries, as before, showed the way in land reclamation. The Dutch had long been reclaiming land from the sea, and they perfected many means of drainage which they taught to British improvers. Marshes and fens, areas of flat, watery land, had been a wilderness used only for fishing, hunting birds, and some grazing since medieval times. Rivers in the fenlands reg-

WATER MEADOWS

One new method that improved British farms was watering meadows. The process involved blocking a stream by building a dam and allowing the backed-up water to completely flood a low-lying meadow. In time, the dam was removed and the waters receded as flow was restored. Damp, silted meadows then produced better grass. In 1826 William Cobbett described water meadows in Wiltshire, in his book William Cobbett's Illustrated Rural Rides: 1821–1832.

Every farm has its portion of down [grassy hills], arable [cropland], and meadows; and in many places, the latter are watered meadows, which is a good resource where sheep are kept in flocks; because these meadows furnish grass for the suckling ewes, early in the spring; and, indeed, because they have always food on them for sheep and cattle of all sorts. These meadows have had no part of the suffering from the drought, this year. They fed the ewes and lambs in the spring, and they are now yielding a heavy crop of hay: for I saw men mowing in them, in several places, particularly about Netheravon, though it was raining at the time.

ularly flooded, and diseases lurked in the marsh. But beginning in the 1600s, and reaching a peak about 1800, the fenland was largely drained and reclaimed for farming. The effort took many generations and involved every level of government, landowners, and engineers. Daniel Defoe described some of the effort in the 1720s:

The history of the draining of those fens, by a set of gentlemen called the Adventurers, the several laws for securing and preserving the banks, and dividing the lands . . . how all the water in this part of England, which does not run into the Thames, the Trent, or the Severn, falls together into these low grounds, and empty themselves into the sea by these drains . . . and how by the skill of these Adventurers, and at a prodigious expence, they have cut new channels, even whole rivers . . . to carry off the great flux of waters . . . all this . . . would take up so much room . . . that I cannot think of entering any farther upon it.

I have only to add, that [on] these fens of Lincolnshire . . . we see innumerable numbers of cattle, which are fed up to an extraordinary size by the richness of the soil.[19]

The fields reclaimed from fens amounted to about 10 percent of England's farmland. On the fields were planted both the usual crops and Dutch-inspired "industrial" crops, including rape for oil, and hemp for making rope, besides the good grass that fed Defoe's cattle.

The new process of draining also helped change the medieval system of ridges and trenches, or furrows, which were meant to drain the land. The opinion of a draining expert was reported in Ireland in 1802:

> He alluded to the practice, which he said had existed from time immemorial, of throwing the land into ridges and furrows, and showed that, by the soil being washed from the tops of the ridges into the furrows, the higher parts of the field produced relatively little crop. . . . In thorough-drained land no drop of water should run on the surface in any direction, but should penetrate into the ground where it fell. . . . Wherever the land was drained, it was necessary that high ridges should be done away with, and the land laid perfectly level.[20]

Another important area of "waste" were the vast English heaths, where thick heathers covered the land for miles. Recovering heath required "paring and burning," a process in which a special plow was used to cut off the vegetation, which was then burned in huge piles, and the ashes spread on the land. Heath soil was poor and had to be enriched with lime and marl (a kind of clay), plus plenty of manure. With proper treatment, the land could and did support highly productive Norfolk system–type farms. A French visitor in 1794 observed that it was only the effort of the improving farmers that made the land yield so well: "The fertility of this land is entirely artificial: the . . . vegetable bed is perhaps no more than eight or ten inches deep, and a few years of bad management would make it as impoverished today as it was before."[21]

By the turn of the century, turning waste land into arable land had become a kind of national mission. The government and the new Board of Agriculture were committed to it. The president of the board, Sir John Sinclair, compared the mission to British military triumphs: "Let us not be satisfied with the liberation of Egypt, or the subjugation of Malta, but let us subdue Finchley Common; let us conquer Hounslow Heath, let us compel Epping Forest to submit to the yoke of improvement."[22]

THE SPIRIT OF IMPROVEMENT

Sir John Sinclair, like other educated Englishmen, was caught up in a feeling called at the time the spirit of improvement. It was an attitude fostered by the Enlightenment, a philosophical movement of the 1700s that used reason to question old ways of doing things and to seek better ones. The Enlightenment in England had a scientific background. Isaac Newton had made many discoveries about the physical world in the 1600s, using only very simple experiments and reason. His work inspired others to rational experimentation, supported by philosopher John Locke, who maintained that people were not born with special knowledge or special sin. Instead, he said, the brain was a "tabula rasa," or a blank sheet of paper. On it could be written whatever the person learned from experience and education. The Enlightenment philosophy held that all people were capable of learning and improving.

Enlightenment thinking also held that God had given the world to man, with the plan that man would use his mind and labor to understand and improve it. The most obvious place to do so was the farm. English poet Oliver Goldsmith called the natural earth a God-sent "habitation." In nature, wrote Goldsmith, some things such as water and edible plants are provided, but others take work:

> While many of [man's] wants are thus kindly furnished, on the one hand, there are numberless inconveniences to excite his industry on the other. This habitation, though provided with all the conveniences of air, pasturage, and water, is but a desert place, without human cultivation.
>
> A world thus furnished with advantages on the one side and inconveniences on the other, is the proper abode of reason, is the fittest to exercise the industry of a free and thinking creature. [23]

In this nineteenth-century painting, a farmer spreads manure to fertilize the soil and increase his crop yield.

Education was essential for human progress, in this view. People needed to learn if they were to make improvements. The British agricultural revolution was accompanied by a flood of educational literature, especially after 1770, when the tireless farm promoter Arthur Young published the results of over five hundred agricultural experiments in his *Farmer's Tours*. Local farmers' associations began to form at the same time. The associations collected information in libraries, hosted speakers, and held farm shows. The twenty-three associations listed in 1803 had increased to over seven hundred by 1855. The national government sponsored a Board of Agriculture in 1793 to record progress on British farms; Arthur Young was made its first head.

THE "VAMPIRE" DISEASE

Pellagra is a disease caused by lack of the nutrient niacin. It became severe in the 1700s in Europe, when maize (American corn) was established as a major food for the poor of Spain, Italy, and the areas north of Italy—including Transylvania. The article "The Origins of Maize: The Puzzle of Pellagra" by the European Food Information Council explains how maize, pellagra, and vampire stories may have become intertwined.

Unfortunately, wherever maize went, a disease called "pellagra" was sure to follow. The connection between maize and pellagra was first described by Casal in Spain in 1735. When it became an epidemic disease in northern Italy, Frencesco Frapoli of Milan named it "pelle agra" (pelle, skin; agra, sour). Chemically, the disease is identified by the three Ds—dermatitis, diarrhea, and dementia [temporary insanity]—and if untreated, pellagra typically leads to death in four or five years.

For years, the lack of medical knowledge and the earlier suspicion that pellagra was caused by some hypothetical toxin in maize, or as a result of infectious agents or a genetic condition, led to major pellagra epidemics in Europe and the United States.

The puzzle started to be solved when it was noticed that pellagra was rare in Mexico despite widespread consumption of maize. The reason appeared to be . . . [that people there] softened the corn to make it edible with an alkaline solution—limewater. This process liberated the bound niacin . . . for digestion.

The knowledge of the chemistry of this process ultimately explained a long standing nutritional puzzle. . . .

There are many who think that the development of beliefs in vampires was associated with pellagra. Just as folklore states that vampires must avoid sunlight to maintain their strength and avoid decay, sufferers from pellagra are hypersensitive to sunlight. Clinical symptoms of pellagra include insomnia, aggression, anxiety, and subsequent dementia, all of which may have contributed to the vampire legends and European folklores of the 1700s.

Agricultural Change Outside England

Information about the Norfolk system and other new ways of handling the land did not spread or catch on quickly outside England and the Low Countries. Other European countries with similar-sized farms, such as France, the German areas, and Italy, eventually did change their farming, but not until fifty to a hundred or more years after the English. The reasons had to do with social and political resistance to change, and the landlords' wish to keep wealth coming as it always had. In France, Louis XIV kept his country at war in spite of famine, even as the first steps toward agricultural improvement were made in England. The Abbe Fenelon, a French priest and outspoken critic of the king, dared to write in the 1690s:

> Your people, Sire, whom you should love as your children, and who up to this time have been so devoted to you, are dying of hunger. The land is left almost unattended, towns and countryside are deserted, trade of all kinds falls off and can no longer support the workers: all commerce is at a standstill. . . . For the sake of getting and keeping vain conquests abroad, you have destroyed half the real strength of your own state. Rather than take money from your poor people, you ought to feed and cherish them. . . . All France is now no more than one great hospital, desolate and unprovided. . . . The people believe you have no pity for their sufferings, that you care only for your own power and glory. They say that if the king had a father's

heart for his people, he would surely think his glory lay rather in giving them bread than in keeping hold of a few frontier posts. [24]

By the mid-1700s some French aristocrats and scholars were taking an interest in the British improvements, and the spirit of the Enlightenment encouraged this. Yet the French made only a few steps toward the British system. In 1761 the French government set up a department of agriculture and encouraged agricultural societies to inform peasants about better farming. Laws were also passed allowing the voluntary redistribution of land to common fields. The laws and news were not much put into practice, though. Historian George F. Rudé gives some likely reasons:

> It seems to have been for a variety of reasons, the most simple being that a great many Frenchmen, either from apathy, fear of peasant revolt, or that their own interests would be injured, ignored or resisted the innovations. Peasant hostility had certainly to be reckoned with: the abolition of grazing rights and 'intercommoning' [agreements by villages to share adjoining commons] was a serious threat to established and treasured village practice . . . but basically . . . it was the tenacity of the small and middling independent proprietor, the *laboureur,* to preserve the old ways against dangerous innovation. [25]

Certainly, there was no trust between the small farmers on the land and the aristocrats promoting the new farming ideas and running the French government.

An Amish farmer tills his Pennsylvania cornfields using draft animals harnessed to a plow. North American farmers were slow to adopt new technology under frontier conditions.

Other parts of Europe were not easily suited to the new farming because of climate or geography. Scandinavia north of Denmark was very cold and rocky; southern Spain was subject to drought and loss of population. To the east, in Russia and in Poland, there was so much land available that landholders felt no need to improve the farms they had. Instead, they sought workers to clear forests and make use of the fer-

tile soil on hand. As one Russian landlord said to his steward, "I don't need more land. I need peasants." [26]

UNIMPROVED FARMS IN NORTH AMERICA

It might be expected that the new methods would catch on quickly in North America, where English immigrants had created so many farms in their own tradition beginning in the mid-1600s. Yet through the 1700s, and longer in the western frontier, the same conditions held in North America as in Russia. There was land aplenty. Why then should farmers work to improve their land? They could simply move on. A Swedish professor of botany, visiting the colonies in 1747, described the kind of farming he saw:

> After the inhabitants have converted into a tillable field a tract of land which was forest for many centuries and which consequently had a very fine soil, they use it as long as it will bear any crops. When it ceases to bear any they turn it into pastures for the cattle and take new grain fields in another place, where a rich black soil can be found that has never been used. . . . Their eyes are fixed upon the present gain, and they are blind to the future.[27]

European visitors like the professor remarked often on the "careless" habits of American farmers, such as leaving big stumps and rocks in fields, or dropping farm work to go hunting or fishing. In fact, though, the farmers were making the best of the resources at hand. Why spend valuable time removing stumps when more land could be plowed by simply enlarging the field? Why even stick to planting when dinner is easier to gain by shooting a deer?

As the Swedish professor predicted, however, the future did catch up with American farmers over time. By 1800 the eastern United States was dotted with rocky, worn-out farms, many of them abandoned by settlers who had gone west to find better land. At last, interest rose in land improvement and in new agricultural implements. It turned out that the American contribution to the agricultural revolution was largely in the form of new tools, inventions that made farming more productive both on old farms and on the vast new lands to the west.

Chapter

3 Technology Speeds the Revolution

In 1731 British lawyer and gentleman farmer Jethro Tull combined some ideas and published them in a work called *Horse Hoeing Husbandry*. Tull's first idea was that the plow could not only break the soil, but it could also plant seeds. His second idea was that the planted furrows should be separated by enough space so that a kind of horse-drawn plow, called a horse hoe, could be used to remove weeds. These machines and methods were far better, he argued, than the "Old Way," from the point of view of "1, the Expense, 2, the Goodness, and 3, the Certainty, of a Crop," not to mention "the Condition in which the Land is left after a Crop."[28] Tull quickly became famous as the inventor of the seed drill and is often mentioned as an important figure in the agricultural revolution. Yet plows, which also planted seeds, were heard of a century before. And fifty years after Tull's "invention," his seed drill was hardly being used anywhere. Nonetheless, with improvements, seed drills did become important and standard tools on British and American farms by the mid-1800s.

The story of Jethro Tull's invention is not unusual. Many inventive ideas put forward in the 1700s had deep roots in the past, and many of them failed to take hold at first; but the new spirit of improvement and Enlightenment did encourage invention. Finally, mostly after 1800, the inventions were reworked and perfected, and new farm machines and implements were produced that actually went into common use. Once they did, the new machines gave farm production an extra push.

THE PACE OF CHANGE

It can be hard for modern people, used to picking up the latest cell phone or computer software, to understand why the pace of technological change was so very, very slow on European and American farms in the 1700s. There were many reasons for it. Farmers, for one thing, tended to be traditional and conservative. They held to the medieval attitude that there were enough risks in the weather and the soil quality, the health of animals, and the habits of harmful pests. Why take a risk on an invention that was unproven? Besides, it was difficult until late in the century for many traditional farmers to find out about new machinery, because little information was available and many farmers could not read. And most farmers had no cash for extras.

Farmers also cultivated a variety of lands in a variety of ways, and what worked in one place did not necessarily work in another. A light plow popular in Britain in the 1700s, for example, was hardly used in the American colonies because it failed against the rough stumps and stones of new fields. In northern Britain, barley and oats were reaped with a sickle, while in southern Britain, they were mowed with a scythe. Why were the customs different? Perhaps southern farmers were better informed (the scythe is more efficient). Or perhaps the sickle in the north made better use of available labor; women traditionally used the sickle but not the scythe.

Certainly, the form of landownership could also slow change. Villagers with common land rights and scattered fields had little reason to spend money on machinery because most tasks were done cooperatively. Tenants or owners of small farms often felt they would not gain enough benefit from new machines, even if they could afford them. Owners of large farms with laborers tended not to want machines as long as human labor was cheap.

Markets and prices were also very important in setting the pace of change. If a farmer could not see that machines would help create a larger harvest which then could be sold at a good profit, the machines were not worth buying.

Against these forces of tradition in the 1700s were set the new ideas of the Enlightenment, described in the last chapter, and an increase in the marketing and trade of agricultural products. Above all, the beginnings of the industrial revolution hurried the pace of technological change on the

An eighteenth-century illustration depicts French farmers sowing seeds in a field tilled by a horse-drawn plow. More efficient plows built of iron were first used in Britain.

farm. In the late 1700s, as the population grew in Europe, more and more people moved to cities and took up work in factories instead of farms. In those factories, for the first time, parts of cast iron, steel, and wood could be produced and assembled quickly and cheaply, in a standard way. Among the products of the new factories were the plows, seed drills, reapers, and threshers that helped make this great shift possible.

PLOWS AND PLOW POWER

At the beginning of the agricultural revolution, plows were heavy and wooden, with wheels set on either side. Iron pieces might be nailed or bolted to the plow at wear points, a job done by the farmer or the local blacksmith. A team of oxen typically pulled the plow, with at least one man or boy to prod or lead them and another man to guide the plow.

Plows without wheels, called swing plows, were first introduced to Britain from Holland, but a dramatic improvement in the swing plow was made by British inventors Disney Stanyforth and Joseph Folljambe in 1730. They patented the Rotherham plow, a lightweight yet strong swing plow that moved through the earth with surprising ease. The reason for that was the shape of the moldboard, the part of the plow which

ACCEPTING THE SEED DRILL

Farmers were slow to accept most new technology. The British landowner Thomas William Coke, Lord Leicester, Earl of Holkham (1752–1842), was famous for getting his tenants to try new things. But the seed drill he favored was not soon used. His great-grandson Thomas Coke tells the story in A.M.W. Stirling's Coke of Norfolk and His Friends.

In an agricultural district any change is regarded with suspicion, and a discovery, even when admitted to be advantageous, is too often allowed to lapse into oblivion rather than be adopted. For sixteen years Coke used the [seed] drill before any one could be induced to do so; even when the farmers at last began to recognize the advantage of the quicker method, he estimated that its use spread only at the rate of a mile a year. "When I introduced the drill," he said afterwards, "it was a long time before I could get a disciple." It used to be said: "Oh, it's very beautiful—and it's very well for *Mr. Coke!*" but that it might be equally well for Mr. Coke's tenants was carefully ignored. By and by, however, he discovered that a quaint term for a good crop of barley had come into use upon the estate. His farmers called it *hat-barley*, for the reason that if a man throws his hat into a crop, the hat rests on the surface if the crop is good, but falls to the ground if it is bad. "*All*, sir," pronounced his tenants at length, "is 'hat-barley' since the drill came!"

helped turn the earth back from the cut made by the point of the plow, called the plowshare. In the Rotherham plow, the plowshare and moldboard were one continuous iron-plated shape. The Rotherham moved so easily that it was possible to reduce the power needed to pull it. This encouraged a changeover in animal power, which was already under way.

Oxen had for centuries been the standard plow pullers, but they were slow. An observer in the British county of Gloucestershire watched teams of men and oxen take seven hours to plow less than an acre: "Many times have I been compelled to look at some tree at a distance to ascertain whether or not the plough-teams were moving."[29] With the lighter swing plow, fewer men and animals were needed. And speed improved greatly with another kind of animal altogether: the horse.

The switch, as it happened on one farm, was recorded in the diary of fifteen-year-old Noah Blake. Daniel was the Blakes' ox, and he worked hard. Noah's diary is full of entries such as "15 [April]: Father used Daniel this morning to set the bridge beams in place. I tried my hand at spring plowing in the afternoon, with Daniel." Then came June 27: "This has been a poor day. Daniel is dead." Noah felt so sad that he and his friend Sarah decided to "plant a fine tree over his grave." Next came a surprise, on the Fourth of July: "Father bought a horse and waggon! We shall collect them on Saturday." First, they

As plows became lighter throughout the 1700s, farmers began using fast-moving horses as draft labor.

had to make ready for the new, lively animal, called Bang: "Father says a horse will jump over such fences as ours so we began making them higher." The liveliness, however, also translated into greater speed: "We went into the village to collect Bang and the waggon. Bang is faster on the road than Daniel; we arrived home in less than ten minutes."[30] Bang was also quicker at the plow.

MORE HORSES PULLING CAST-IRON PLOWS

Noah Blake's diary was written in 1805, on an American farm, but the same experience had been repeated on countless farms in Europe during the previous century. Horsepower took over from oxen, and as it did so, more horses were raised and bred for farm purposes. Between 1700 and 1850, the number of horses in Britain doubled, and the amount of horsepower available to each farmworker grew by a third in the 1700s alone. At the same time, farm implements were designed with horsepower in mind.

Plow improvement took another leap with the work of Robert Ransome of Ipswich, England. He introduced hardened cast-iron plowshares in the 1780s, and by 1808 was offering standardized parts for easy replacement. Cast-iron plows made in a foundry replaced the parts and plates turned out by local smiths. In 1840, the Ransome factory was turning out eighty-six different kinds of cast-iron plows to suit local needs. William Cobbett, traveling through the countryside in 1821, found a farmer with an up-to-date plow "plowing" while simply guiding his horses, in a way that predicted the future. The "coulter" he mentions was another improvement, a kind of wheeled blade that aided the action of the plow itself:

> Returned this morning and rode about the farm, and also about that of Mr. WINNAL, where I saw, for the first time, a plough going about *without being held.* The man drove the three horses that drew the plough, and carried the plough round at the ends; but left it to itself the rest of the time. There was a skim coulter that turned the sward in under the furrow; and the work was done very neatly. This gentleman has six acres of cabbages. . . . He has weighed one of what he deemed an average weight, and found it to weigh fifteen pounds without the stump. Now, as there are 4,320

upon an acre, the weight of the acre is *thirty tons* all but 400 pounds! This is a prodigious crop.[31]

SEEDING AND WEEDING

Jethro Tull's idea that seed should be distributed selectively to the furrow, instead of "broadcast" out by hand, was sound. Seed drilling used only about 30 percent of the amount used in broadcasting, to produce the same crop in similar conditions. By 1800, at last, the seed drill was established in some British counties. But Tull's other idea, the horse hoe, was less popular. Basically, it was a plow intended to displace weeds between rows of plants, but it did this job so poorly that one French agricultural expert advised farmers to avoid it and instead hoe by hand. Such "improvements" made before 1766 did not impress one mechanic:

> For the mechanism of those [horse hoes] devised hitherto, by ingenious lovers of agriculture, is of so perplexed, and complicated a nature, that it will no ways answer the common purposes of husbandry: but, being perpetually out of order, will throw the poor ploughman into despondancy . . . as neither he, nor the country plough-wright, can comprehend how to remedy any defects, or accidents, except with extreme difficulty.[32]

This criticism could be applied to many well-meaning inventions of the period: until standardized parts were available, any machine of much complexity was devilishly hard to repair. Not until after 1850 did a good, simplified horse-drawn hoe with teeth (instead of a plowlike share) make its appearance on British farms.

British Harvest Inventions

The greatest amount of labor on the farm was spent in gathering and processing the harvest. Even though there was a great need for machinery to help with the harvest, reaping improvements were slow to come. Reaping by hand advanced from the sickle, a curved serrated-edge knife, to the smooth-edged hook and "bagging" hook (which collected grain as it was used to cut), to the large two-handed scythe. Before 1750, sickle reaping was most common all over Britain. Scythes were used only in some places. The change began in the south, and moved northward, possibly because of labor shortages. Sickle reaping took an average of four worker-days per acre, while scythe reaping took only two and a half. Efforts to invent a workable reaping machine failed until 1812, when a millwright named John Common designed a horse-drawn reaper, which became the basis of the successful American McCormick reaper. The McCormick did not arrive in Britain until the Great Exhibition held in London in 1851, when it gained instant fame and European success.

Horse Plowing

The art of hand plowing with horses remained a memory for three American farmers who spoke to sociologist Douglas Harper at the turn of the twenty-first century. He recorded these and other memories of farm change in his book Changing Works: Visions of a Lost Agriculture.

Arthur: A good pair of horses, you can do an acre and a half a day. Maybe a little more, dependin' on how good the ground is. How many stones are in it. I have plowed two acres a day. But then I had a good start. I had a better team than these fellows, maybe. Stones . . . what happens when you hit 'em? Well, up in the air come them handles . . . up in the air! They might hit your chest . . . your chin. Got to go slow and then back up and pull it back and start over again!

Willie: You move with the plow. When you hit a stone it picks you right off the ground—I was small and it picked me right off the ground. Your plow is set so it will go into the ground—there is a little wheel which keeps it from going too far—a leveler wheel called a colter. You set this for your depth; if your plow was going too deep, you set the wheel down. It's not a big effort to do that.

Jim Carr: If you want nice plowin' you get somebody that can plow with a hand plow. They'll lay that baby right over and it'll be just as true as can be. You're going the same speed—you're not going fast. And she'll just roll her right over. When you look across the field all your furrows are just right.

Threshing and winnowing went on for months in the barn after the actual harvest. One commentator describes the pace of this "dressing": "The operation of dressing was slow. As the sun streamed through a crack in the barn-door, it reached the notches which were cut in the wood-work to mark the passage of time and the recurrence of the hours for lunch and dinner. The operation was expensive as well as slow, costing from six to seven shillings a quarter."[33]

Various machines were invented to take advantage of horsepower to save time and money in the barn. The model for them was the horse-powered flour mill, called a "gingeng" (meaning back-and-forth) in the north. The horse, hitched to a beam, walked in a circle around a device containing a millstone, which was made to turn by a set of gears attached to the beam. Winnowing fans and kinds of threshers were powered the same way. A breakthrough invention was the thresher of Andrew Meikle of Scotland in 1786. His machine threshed and winnowed, and its usage quickly spread south into the rest of Britain. One reason was that

Invented in the early nineteenth century, the horse-drawn McCormick reaper revolutionized the harvesting process, the most labor-intensive phase of cereal farming.

it could be powered by hand, by horse, by water, or even by steam.

A variety of other machines were perfected around 1800, including root slicers, straw or chaff cutters, and feed crushers. All benefited from greater use of iron, standardized parts, and increased publicity. A psychological momentum also developed on the changing farms: when one device was seen to work, the farmer and his neighbor were more interested in trying the next new thing.

THE SPIRIT OF IMPROVEMENT IN AMERICA

In America, following the Revolutionary War, many wealthy, educated landholders—gentleman farmers—were eager for their new country to take its place in the world as a home of advanced ideas and abundance. U.S. president James Madison wrote down in 1819 the most important fact about early North American farming: "Whilst there was an abundance of fresh and fertile soil, it was the interest of the cultivator to spread his labor over as great a surface as he could. Land being cheap and labour dear [expensive], and the land co-operating powerfully with the labour, it was profitable to draw as much as possible from the land." [34] It seemed to Madison that their abundant land should benefit from agricultural improvements that were suited to it. Primary among the possible improvements were machines and tools that could permit fewer laborers to produce more.

Madison may have gained his enthusiasm from the first American president. In the 1780s, George Washington ordered two of the most modern plows from Britain and a threshing machine. His new plows had little impact, and when they broke, they were difficult to repair. The threshing machine, too, was disappointing. Washington tried building his own and working with American versions of threshing machines, but in 1793, he declared, "I have seen so much of beginning and ending of new inventions, that I have almost resolved to go on in the old way of treading." [35] By "treading" he meant having livestock trample the grain to thresh it—with the accompanying problem of dealing with the animals' droppings. Still, Washington kept up his practical efforts at mechanical improvement, and even invented a "seed drill," which was actually a barrel with holes in it. The worker was supposed to roll the barrel along the field, allowing the seeds to fall from the barrel's holes into the furrow.

Washington's eagerness for improvement was more than matched by Thomas Jefferson. He imported the best plants he could find from Europe for his gardens and farm and remained certain that agricultural machinery could be perfected. In 1784, after observing plows in the French town of Nancy, Jefferson decided that the proper curve of a plow's moldboard could be determined mathematically. His calculations led to plow designs, and even though the math did not predict the best curve, he was willing to make practical changes. Jefferson used his own plows on his land after 1794. He also promoted, and possibly helped design, a hillside plow built by his son-in-law. To show how good Jefferson's plow designs were, he was eager to use the dynamometer,

George Washington on American Farmers' "Bad Habits"

Eager to do a good job at Mount Vernon, George Washington carried on a correspondence with Arthur Young, the British promoter of farm improvement. His letters are collected in an 1847 book, Letters on Agriculture from His Excellency, George Washington. *In this letter, Washington tries to explain to Young why American farming of the 1790s produces so little per acre.*

Philadelphia, December 5, 1791

An English farmer must entertain a contemptible opinion of our husbandry, or a horrid idea of our lands, when he shall be informed that not more than eight or ten bushels of wheat is the yield of an acre; but this low produce may be ascribed, and principally too, to a cause . . . namely, that the aim of the farmer in this country (if they can be called farmers) is, not to make the most they can from the land, which is, or has been, cheap; but the most of the labour, which is dear [expensive]; the consequence of which has been, much ground has been *scratched* over and none cultivated or improved as it ought to have been; whereas a farmer in England, where land is dear, and labour cheap, finds it in his interest to improve and cultivate highly, that he may reap large crops from a small quantity of ground. That the last is true, and the first an erroneous policy, I will readily grant; but it requires time to conquer bad habits, and hardly any thing short of necessity is able to accomplish it. That necessity is approaching by pretty rapid strides.

a device invented in Britain to measure the amount of pull needed to move a plow through the earth. But he was unable to get one due to hostilities leading into the War of 1812 between Britain and the United States.

The fever of improvement on the part of these famous leaders and some other American enthusiasts made little difference in American farm performance between the American Revolution (1775–1783) and the War of 1812 (1812–1815). Parts or replacements for imported machines were hard to get and were expensive. Even homegrown inventions inspired little trust. Few farmers were convinced that new implements would actually improve their yield. Many were still close to the colonial experience, when a few casual pokes in the ground with a digging stick was enough to prepare a cornfield. And some plantation owners thought that slaves worked best with simple tools.

More Fertile Grounds for Inventions

Following the War of 1812, a number of factors led to a flurry of agricultural inventions in the United States. The Northwest Territory, the old frontier land of the colonies, had been pulling would-be farmers from the East since the Revolution. So many had settled there that the territory was already turning into a set of states. People began to shift into the newly opened Louisiana Territory, bought by Jefferson in 1803. Back East, fewer hands were available to work, and some farms had worn out from overuse of the soil. Farmers in those regions were especially eager to find labor-saving devices and ways to improve their land. At the same time, the industrial revolution was reaching into America, as it did into Britain. By the 1830s, factories with machine tools were capable of turning out inexpensive standardized parts for machines. The inventions of people like Jefferson could finally be produced cheaply, and repaired with replacement parts.

Other encouragement for new farm technology came from American agricultural societies. Some of these were first founded after the Revolutionary War, but they tended to count only gentleman farmers as their members. The information they spread about improved farming was largely imported from England. Farmers seeking a real profit often felt, as one man said, that the societies' advice had "a tendency to render tillage and pasturage more showy than useful." [36] Later, though, more practical societies were founded, often with state support. A model for them was the Berkshire Agricultural Society, established in 1811. Its founder, Elkanah Watson, organized one of the first livestock fairs where animals, farm produce, and handcrafts were exhibited, accompanied by social events and entertainment. The *Weekly Register* newspaper noted Watson's influence in 1819:

The public newspapers teem with accounts of shows and fairs, and the proceedings of the numerous societies which have sprung from their common parent in Berkshire, Mass. to immortalize the venerable name of Watson, and disseminate useful facts into every district of our country. The best methods of managing a farm, in all its details, rearing cattle, sheep and swine, etc., and of applying the surplus labor of the people within doors, are carefully attended to, and every man's experience is thrown into the common stock of knowledge—the *power* thereby to be acquired is of incomprehensible magnitude. [37]

The societies' fairs were the ancestors of today's American county and state fairs, with

Today's county and state fairs in America evolved from the livestock fairs organized by Massachusetts' Berkshire Agricultural Society in the 1800s.

their agricultural emphasis and their atmosphere of fun. The societies actively encouraged farm improvement through their journals, and they offered prizes for good solutions to agricultural problems. Many of those challenges led to invention. And the prize-winning inventions gained publicity and public acceptance when they were exhibited at the agricultural fairs.

Finally, advertisements in society journals, fair demonstrations, traveling salesmen, and farm supply stores drove up demand for money-saving inventions. Manufacturers of farm implements mushroomed between 1815 and 1850 as the business became more and more profitable. Historian Peter D. McClelland argues that the economic aspect of farm improvement was actually more important in the United States than in Britain:

> From first to last [the American agricultural revolution] was little affected or directed by the American [version] of the British squire, with idle time and abundant funds to investigate elaborate contrivances with questionable economic pay-offs. This revolution was determined by the market, and its participants, by and large, were preoccupied with profits: inventors and manufacturers striving to make money, and potential customers anxious to save money in the operation of their farms and plantations. It was, in short, a revolution that was quintessentially capitalistic in motivation and American in character. [38]

AMERICAN PLOWS

In the fifteen years following the War of 1812, 127 patents were granted for new designs of American plows—ten times the number in the previous fifteen years. Manufactured iron parts were vital to these designs, as inventors vied to create the best product. Jethro Wood of New York patented an all-cast-iron plow in 1814 (improved in 1819), which became famous; but he was not the first American to create one. Another cast-iron plow patented in 1797 had no success because suspicious farmers claimed that the cast iron poisoned the ground and made weeds grow. It is possible that both Wood and the inventor of this earlier plow knew about Ransome's cast-iron plow in Britain, but it is not certain. In any case, by Wood's day, the poisoning idea was dead (thanks at least in part to the work of the agricultural societies). Wood described his new plow in his patent application. Note that Wood is eager to reject the old kind of wooden plow with wrought iron plates:

> In the first place, the said Jethro Wood claims an exclusive privilege for constructing the part of the Plough . . . generally called the mould-board. . . . This mould-board may be termed a plano-curvilinear figure, not defined nor described in any of the elementary books of geometry or mathematics. . . . The figure of the mould-board, as observed from the furrow-side, is a sort of irregular pentagon, or five-sided plane, though curved and inclined in a peculiar manner. . . . In the second place, the said Jethro Wood claims an exclusive right and privilege in the construction of a standard of cast iron . . . for connecting the mould-board with the beam. . . . In the third place, the said Jethro Wood claims an exclusive privilege in

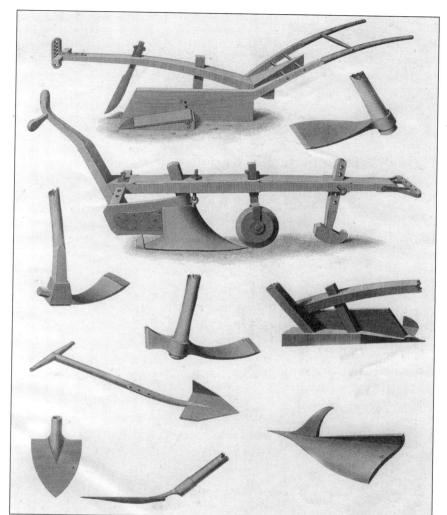

the inventions and improvements made by him in the construction of the cutting edge of the mould-board, or what may be called, in plain language, the plowshare. . . .

The said inventor and petitioner wishes it to be understood, that the principal metallic material of his Plough is cast iron. He has very little use for wrought iron, and by adapting the former to the extent he has done, and by discontinu-ing the latter, he is enabled to make the Plough stronger and better, as well as more lasting and cheap. [39]

While the plow's cast iron was a selling point, even more important to its popularity was the fact that it was made of three cast-iron pieces, which could be replaced by new parts if necessary.

A variety of plow improvements followed Wood's, including moldboards that not only turned the soil over but shaped it in a kind of screw which allowed for more air to be mixed with the earth. No plow, however, was up to the job American settlers faced when they first tried to farm the prairie soil of the Great Plains. Prairie soil was extremely heavy and sticky, and the natural grasses formed thick roots. Plows failed to cut through, got stuck, or broke in midfield. In 1837, John Deere, a blacksmith in Grand Detour, Illinois, created a workable prairie plow by attaching a steel share to a wrought-iron moldboard and by grinding both very smooth. He advertised his invention in 1843:

> John Deere respectfully informs his friends and customers, the agricultural community, of this and adjoining counties, and dealers in Ploughs, that he is now prepared to fill orders for the same on presentation.
>
> The Mouldboard of his well, and so favorably known PLOUGH, is made of wrought iron, and the share of steel, ⁵⁄₁₆ of an inch thick, which carries a fine sharp edge. The whole face of the mold board and share is ground smooth, so that it scours perfectly bright in any soil, and it will not choke in the foulest of ground. It will do more work in a day, and do it much better and with less labor, to both team and holder, than the ordinary ploughs that do not scour, and in consequence of the ground being better prepared, the agriculturalist obtains a much heavier crop.[40]

Deere's plow permitted farms to be built on the Great Plains. Without it, the government probably would not have opened the northern prairie land to settlers with the Homestead Act (1862); and the network of farms connected by railways would not have developed there, which led to the growth of the city of Chicago.

AMERICAN WAYS WITH MACHINES

Other farm machinery evolved in particularly American ways. Efforts to make seed drills that would deliver seeds to furrows were not very successful (as Jethro Tull's was not) because of the tricky feed mechanism. It was not until after 1850 that this problem was resolved. However, American inventors took their own direction in creating sowing machines that imitated hand broadcast sowing. Particularly successful was Bennett's of 1816, a long box set on a kind of wheelbarrow, with little revolving brushes that sent the seed out small holes in the box. The device was adapted for horse pulling in 1822. American farmers seem to have liked it because it allowed quick and even sowing of tiny seeds, which were hard to spread well by hand.

The English horse hoe was altered in the hands of Americans to become the "cultivator," a triangle-shaped device with teeth for taking out weeds between rows. A wide variety of threshers and winnowers developed by the 1830s, many using the power of a horse on a treadmill; at least one depended on a dog treadmill. Perhaps the greatest American farm machine triumph before 1850, however, was the mechanical reaper.

Harvest time is the most anxious time of year for any farmer. Ripe grain must be gathered when ripe but not sunburned. Rain at the wrong time can ruin it. Speed in harvesting, therefore, is very important, and large numbers of people had to be assembled in time to do the work before the mechanical reaper appeared.

It is likely that John Common's British reaper was known in North America, from literature at least, when the first American reaper inventor, Obed Hussey of Ohio, patented his invention in 1833. In the next year, Virginian Cyrus McCormick patented his own design. Both men kept improving their machines and vying with one another at agricultural fairs. First, one machine would win at a contest, and then the other. Finally, McCormick's reaper gained the greatest fame

as he moved his manufacturing to Chicago (where he could better serve plains farmers). And he scored wonderful publicity when his reaper was chosen to appear in the Great Exhibition of 1851 in London.

PROCESSING AND POWER

In Britain, and later in the rest of Europe and North America, mechanized processing of agricultural products helped create a market for farmers. The first and most important industrial advances used cotton and wool to make textiles. Weaving, done traditionally by families in cottages, was mechanized in

Before the introduction of the horse-drawn reaper, farmers used handheld implements to harvest grain. Such tools were very cumbersome and slowed grain production.

Britain after the invention of the flying shuttle in the 1730s, followed by the power loom in 1787. Spinning of cotton for the loom was transformed by Lewis Paul's and John Wyatt's spinning machine (1738), followed by the spinning jenny, which increased production by eight times. Meanwhile, still in Britain, Thomas Newcomen built the first piston steam engine in 1705, and improved designs by other British inventors followed, through 1802. The steam engine was to power many of the factories that bought wool and cotton from farmers. The engine was also used in barns in Britain and in America by the 1840s to run threshers and other processing machines. Eventually, in the fields it would power huge "combines," which reaped, threshed, winnowed, and sorted the grain all at once—but that was not until later in the 1800s.

In North America, power from rivers was used for the first factories in the early 1800s. Francis C. Lowell, who founded famous textile mills in Massachusetts, learned his business at a model town in Scotland. Some of the first industrial employees of the United States were former farm girls in New England. By 1840, there were twelve

An illustration shows slaves using Eli Whitney's cotton gin. The machine efficiently separated the seeds from the fibers of short staple cotton.

hundred cotton mills in the United States, and a comparable number of woolen mills. Invention of the sewing machine in the 1840s gave the mills themselves bigger markets.

The cotton business was thriving because of one key invention of 1793: American Eli Whitney's cotton gin. This machine separated the seeds from the fibers of short staple cotton—a job that was so time-consuming for workers that it was hardly worth growing the cotton before the invention of the gin. Whitney wrote, "One man and one horse will do more than fifty men with the old machines."[41] Suddenly, cotton plantations became much more profitable, and planters looked eagerly for new land and new workers. The slave trade, nearly dead before, took on new life. Plantations were established west of the old South, in Alabama and beyond.

The industrial revolution also widened markets for farm goods because it led to new forms of transportation and preservation of food. Steamships and steam trains were at work before 1850. The process of canning food, invented by Frenchman François Appert in 1809, offered a way to save and sell more fruit and vegetables than people could eat immediately. These and other inventions kept increasing the amount farmers could sell, if they could only increase production. The idea of greater profit within reach led many farmers to try the new methods and new machines of the agricultural revolution.

In 1829 one American commentator remarked, "Our farmers are acquiring the first requisites for improvement: a consciousness that their practice is *not* the best, and that they really *want* information. . . . Our implements have been multiplied: and they are better made, and better used than formerly."[42] Both farmers and makers of implements had come to expect, as a matter of course, that farming would keep improving and that farm technology would keep bringing new advantages. This change in attitude was one great accomplishment of the agricultural revolution.

4 Landholding and Marketing Transformed

The fresh farming ideas of the agricultural revolution would have had little effect in Britain—and so little effect elsewhere—had they not been accompanied by important changes in the way land was controlled, and the way farm products were marketed. In general, these changes were part of a great transformation in European history, from economic patterns owing much to old feudal ways to modern capitalism.

Capitalism is the economic system in which each person acts as an independent economic unit, free to earn, buy, and sell goods and labor. The main ideas of capitalism were first expressed in the 1700s. They fit in well with the Enlightenment idea that each individual is born with certain rights and capabilities. In Britain, Adam Smith wrote a key book about capitalism, *The Wealth of Nations*, published in 1776. He argued that mankind had gone through four economic stages. The first and most primitive was that of hunters, in which there was hardly any privately owned property. The second stage was one of shepherds, led by chieftains. The chieftains claimed territory and set themselves up as better than their followers. The third stage was one of farmers, but they were still dominated by leaders who were now feudal lords and landowners. The fourth stage, which Smith claimed had only arrived in his century, was that of commercial activity. This stage was one of freedom for individuals to choose how they were to earn and spend their money. This economic freedom, said Smith, was brought about when such feudal holdovers as dictatorial landowners, tithes and taxes, and especially restraints on trade, were done away with. The result was to be a "revolution of the greatest importance to the publick happiness."[43]

Smith's version of history is far from complete, but his ideas had a great impact. Smith justified the notion that private property and the worker's right to move and take any job were the basis of wealth and happiness. On the farm in Britain, this belief helped propel an end to common fields, a changeover in farm labor, and the growth of the marketing system.

ENCLOSURE

An important British change in landholding that accompanied the agricultural revolution is called enclosure. Generally speaking, enclosure involved making property more private. Lands formerly held or used in common were converted to the use of only the owner or the renter. Land taken out of common use was generally fenced or hedged: it was "enclosed" to keep outsiders off. Enclosure could actually include several processes: establishing new leaseholds (agreements giving one person rights to a piece of land); removing common property rights; changes in farmland layouts and boundaries; combining farms; and extreme changes in land use. Not all enclosures were the same. Some created large combined farms, for example, while others created many small farms.

Enclosure in Britain can be divided into roughly two types. The first was generally done by large landowners before 1700 and involved court actions. Most lords seeking enclosure were trying to get rid of unprofitable villages on their land, with the goal of increasing pasture land or creating new, more profitable leases. Efforts to enclose did not always succeed, though, because villagers were protected by an act of Parliament that made it illegal to depopulate the land. Still, landowners had power and money behind them, and most enclosure efforts went through.

Parliamentary enclosure became the rule in the 1700s and 1800s. If requested by four-fifths of landowners, the lord of the manor, and the owner of the tithe in a given place, Parliament would pass an act of enclosure. A clerk and a surveyor were appointed to carry out the act on the ground. In some ways, this process was more open and fair than the enclosure carried out by lords and courts. Enclosure promised to farmers, including those who only leased their land, the chance to produce more. Nathaniel Kent,

Cows graze on farmland in Yorkshire, England. By the mid–nineteenth century, most of Britain's farmland was privately owned and enclosed by means of stone fences and other barriers.

writing about Norfolk in 1794, explained the connection between farm improvement and enclosure. He began by comparing the work of a farmer with scattered strips of land in a common fields village with the farmer on enclosed land:

Land, when very much divided, occasions considerable loss of time to the occupier, in going over a great deal of useless space, in keeping a communication with the different pieces. As it lies generally in long narrow slips, it is but seldom it can receive any benefit from cross ploughing and harrowing, therefore it cannot be kept so clear [of weeds]; but what is still worse, there can be but lit-

ENCLOSURE AT SHERINGTON

A.C. Chibnall, historian of the village of Sherington in Buckinghamshire, tells the story of what happened in that village at the time of enclosure in 1797 in his book, Sherington.

Sir John Buchanan Riddell's land at Sundon near Luton had been recently enclosed with advantage and at his suggestion the Mercers [major landowners in Sherington] agreed in July 1795 to join the other principal proprietors in an appeal to Parliament for authority "to divide and enclose the Common Fields of Sherington." The necessary act was passed the following year.

The Enclosure commissioners made a detailed valuation of every holding. . . . The arrangement at the time seemed equable to all concerned. . . .

The Enclosure Award was dated 4 July 1797. The resetting of the old common fields seems to have been done effectively, the strong wheat lands in the south being consolidated with a few essentially arable farms and the drier lands to the north distributed with the meadows among a number of dairy farms.

As was apparent from earlier evidence few of the cottagers could show the commissioners a valid title to common rights and only four smallholders were given allotments. Forty-five cottagers retained the garden within which their dwelling was built, but this seldom extended more than half a rood, while 25 others—representing the old squatters on the waste—were allowed no more than the few poles of land upon which their mean cottage stood. All the [benefits] that might have been available to these folk in the old open fields were thus withdrawn without any attempt being made to give them satisfaction in other ways. The re-arrangement of the fields, moreover, made for more efficient farming and in time there was a reduced demand for labour so that many of the hands became redundant [unnecessary] and were forced to seek help through the parish rates [the means of aid to the poor].

tle variety observed in the system of cropping; because the right which every parishioner has of commonage over the field, a great part of the year, prevents the sowing of turnips, clover, or other grass seeds, and consequently cramps a farmer in the stock which he would otherwise keep. On the contrary, when land is inclosed, so as to admit of sowing turnips and seeds, which have an improving and meliorating tendency, the same soil will, in the course of a few years, make nearly double the return it did before, to say nothing of the wonderful improvements which sometimes result from a loam or clay, which will, when well laid down, often become twice the permanent value in pasture, that ever it would as ploughed ground. [44]

Not every enclosed farm was a success, but enough did well to encourage landowners to enclose. Some of the most successful farmers were not actually landowners, but tenant farmers paying new higher rents for enclosed land. The thinking landlord would do his best to make sure tenants could pay the high rent by encouraging the new farming methods, lending money for new machinery or improvements, and even paying the cost of fencing, ditching, or hedging to create the enclosure.

The major burst of parliamentary enclosure happened in Britain after 1750, and this time coincides with the greatest increase in farm production and productivity (amount grown per acre). By 1850, nearly all the cropland of Britain was in private hands, and so was most of the pasture.

In the process of enclosure, the last medieval institutions related to the land faded. Tithes to the church were often removed from landholding at the time of enclosure. People no longer had a right to use of land for pasturing a cow or gathering berries just because they had been born in a local village. In fact, village communities sometimes faded altogether as farmers set their homes not in the central village but out on the farms they now held exclusively. The lord of the manor was no longer responsible for the welfare of "his" people. The idea of "noblesse oblige," meaning the obligation of a nobleman to maintain the people under his domain, faded as a practical rule. So, on the other hand, did the obligation of the villager to serve his lord in ways other than rent payment.

IMPROVEMENT AND ENCLOSURE IN NORTH AMERICA AND EUROPE

Private landownership was the rule almost from the beginning of settlement of North America. The Puritan settlements on the Massachusetts coast did begin as common fields villages, but quickly faded to private ownership. Governor William Bradford of Plymouth described how his fellow settlers left the village to establish their own profitable properties:

For now as their stocks increased, and the increase vendible [marketable], there was no longer any holding them together, but now they must of necessity go to their own great lots. They could not otherwise keep their cattle, and having oxen grown they must have land for plowing and tillage. And no man now thought he could live except he had cattle and a great deal of ground to keep them, all striving to increase their stocks. By which means they were scattered all over the Bay quickly and the town in which they had lived compactly till now was left very thin and in a short time almost desolate. [45]

The common fields villages disappeared both because there was free land all around and because it was possible to sell extra produce (the "increase vendible") for a profit. These factors also worked against the so-called utopian communities of the 1800s in America. These were often founded as religion-based villages with common fields, where people hoped to achieve a more perfect life. Yet within a few generations, most had faded because private farming, with its lure of profit, was so easy to do and so favored by most Americans.

Holland had a tradition of privately held farms before enclosure got under way in Britain. The rest of Europe, however, had barely begun to remove the common system by 1800. For the most part, the powerful landowners resisted change and were backed by the law. In central Europe in 1821, for example, peasant farmers knew they could improve production by planting turnips or clover instead of leaving fields fallow. But, they said, they were "not allowed to . . . [because] the lord has the right of grazing sheep, and as long as there is stubble grazing, we have to let the fallow lie." [46] In Würtemberg, Germany, the church kept farmers from planting the fodder crops because only profits from grains were tithed.

Meanwhile, their prince wanted them to grow sour, unprofitable wine grapes because he could collect taxes on them.

In some cases, village communities also resisted change. Strong communities in western Germany, for example, refused to sell any land to outsiders. Even in France after the French Revolution, when farming began to improve, the Marquess of Marboef was sentenced to death by a people's tribunal for taking land away from traditional crops to grow the new fodder crops.

It was not until late in the 1700s that agricultural experiments with British and Dutch methods began in some regions of France, Switzerland, Denmark, and western Germany. And the change did not come until the later nineteenth or even twentieth century in Russia and eastern Europe. There, the great power of the lords had actually increased in the 1600s and 1700s, as they gained more serfs and more land. Serfdom did not encourage farm improvement. Between 1750 and 1799, the average ratio of seed harvested to seed planted is estimated at 10.1 in Britain and Holland, and 7 in France, Spain, and Italy. In Russia, it was 4.7.

SERFDOM AND SLAVERY

One reason for low productivity in Russia and other parts of eastern Europe was the use of serfs on vast estates. By 1797 nearly half of all Russians were serfs, working two or three days a week for their lord, or paying heavy dues. In spite of the low productivity of their lands, the lords had so much territory and so many workers that they themselves became very rich by selling their

Farm fields in Burgundy, France, appear like a patchwork quilt when viewed from the air. They reflect the fact that commons system farming ended across Europe in the 1800s.

grain all over Europe. It was not until 1861 that Alexander II of Russia abolished serfdom in Russia because he was threatened by serious peasant revolts. He also realized that industry could never grow in a country without a free labor force. Freedom for serfs in Russian-controlled Poland followed a few years later.

On the islands of the West Indies, on plantations of the American South, and in South America, slaves became important as farmworkers in the 1600s and 1700s. Like serfs,

the slaves produced crops very inexpensively because they cost little to keep. Their labor certainly helped enrich plantation owners and merchants, many of them located far away in Holland, Britain, and France. But slave labor on farms was not part of the agricultural revolution. In fact, the improvements and machinery of that revolution were for the most part ignored on slave plantations (with the distinct exception of the cotton gin). As Ralph Waldo Emerson put it, slavery "does not improve

With the exception of the cotton gin, the improvements resulting from the agricultural revolution had virtually no impact on the farming practices of slave plantations.

the soil, everything goes to decay."[47] However, the products and trade generated by slave labor provided money (capital), which helped to speed the agricultural revolution and the industrial revolution. Before the Civil War, nearly all cotton supplying northern mills in the United States came from slave plantations; and so did 70 percent of the cotton processed in British textile factories.

Enlightenment ideals of liberty and human dignity helped lead to the French Revolution of 1789. Although the aftermath of the Revolution was bloody, the new government followed its slogan of "liberty, equality, fraternity" by ending slavery in 1794 (and in French colonies in 1848). The plantations and trade of the French West Indies finally faded in value. Battles for independence from Spain led to an end to slavery in most of South America by 1830 (although Brazil held out until 1888). A long debate led to abolition in Britain and its possessions as of 1833. In the United States, the economic value of slavery on Southern plantations was made clear when civil war was needed to end it by 1865.

MORE SELLING, AND MORE WAYS TO SELL

As farmers produced more than they needed to feed their families, and as the population grew, methods of selling farm produce expanded. The old local British market, meant to distribute needed food to those who could not grow it themselves, was no longer good enough. More and more middlemen appeared, people who would buy from a farmer in order to resell goods elsewhere. Because of the rules and taxes of the open market, farmers tended to meet middlemen at an inn, bringing along samples of their grain to show its quality. In time, buildings for such trade were erected, such as the 1750 London Corn Exchange. In some towns, the market itself turned into a kind of corn exchange. Daniel Defoe described the activity at such a place:

> Instead of the vast number of horses and wagons of corn on market days there were crowds of farmers, with their samples, and buyers such as mealmen, millers, corn-buyers, brewers etc., thronging the market; and on the days between markets the farmers carried their corn to the hoys [boats or barges used to ship grain] and received their pay.[48]

The old rules restricting trade at open markets and fairs were thus set aside, or used only in times of poor harvests and high prices.

Middlemen, nicknamed "badgers," "kidders," or "jobbers," were traditionally viewed with suspicion as profiteers who contributed little for their pay. However, as their numbers and usefulness grew, they gained more respect. Old laws against middlemen, some

As crop harvests and sales expanded throughout the 1700s, structures such as the Corn Exchange in Kent, England, were built to house large-scale buying and selling of grain.

of which had been on the books for a very long time, were repealed by Parliament in 1772. One result of the rise of middlemen was the fading of fairs and markets in general. The traveling journalist William Cobbett noted this in 1826 and complained bitterly about the rise of middlemen and shops at the expense of fairs:

> [Hambledon] was formerly a considerable market-town, with three fairs in the year . . . [but now] the fairs amount to little more than a couple, or three gingerbread-stalls, with dolls and whistles for children. . . . What are the shop and shop-keeper for? To receive and distribute the produce of the land. There are other articles, certainly; but the main part is the produce of the land. The shop must be paid for; the shop-keeper must be kept; and the one must be paid for and the other must be kept by the consumer of the produce: or, perhaps, partly by the consumer and partly by the producer.
>
> When fairs were very frequent, shops were not needed. . . . Does not everyone see, in a minute, how this exchanging of fairs, and markets, for shops creates *idlers* and *traffickers*; creates those locusts, called middlemen, who create *nothing*, who improve nothing, but who live in idleness, and who live well, too, out of the labor of the producer, and the consumer. The fair and the market, those wise institutions of our forefathers, and with regard to the management of which they were so scrupulously careful; the fair, and the market, bring the producer, and the consumer, in contact with each other . . . and enable them to act for their mutual interest and convenience.[49]

Only six hundred British towns held open markets by 1750. Some markets and fairs became more specialized, dealing only in one product such as cattle, and this helped them survive.

International trade, especially in grain, also increased. Beginning in the 1600s, the British government sought to support its own farmers and traders through a policy called mercantilism. Under that policy, imports were limited and exports of grain were subsidized. Government subsidy for grain meant the government paid part of the cost of the grain, making it less expensive for foreign buyers. The idea was that foreign customers would buy so much British grain that the volume would make up for the low price. Acts of Parliament carrying out the policy were called the Corn Laws. Landowners generally favored the Corn Laws, but in the early 1800s, more and more opposition arose, especially among merchants and industrialists who thought a free market, without government aid, was important for all trade. An Anti–Corn Law League was formed to oppose the laws, and finally in 1846 a bill was written to end them.

INVESTMENTS RETURN TO THE FARM

Increasing trade meant that more farm products could be sold, so that investing in farm improvement seemed like a better and better way to make a profit. In Holland and England, loans became available to farmers at lower interest rates than anywhere else in the world. Adam Smith himself argued that agriculture was the most important cre-

THE BRITISH ECONOMY IN PERSPECTIVE

Economic historian Joel Mokyr explains in The British Industrial Revolution *that British trade in agricultural and other goods was in fact less regulated than that in most of Europe, in spite of the policy of controls on foreign trade.*

Compared with Prussia, Spain, or the Hapsburg Empire, Britain's government generally left its businessmen in peace to pursue their affairs subject to certain restraints and rarely ventured itself into commercial and industrial enterprises. Seventeenth-century mercantilism had placed obstacles in the path of enterprising individuals, but British obstacles were less formidable than those in France. . . . Mercantilism and regulation in eighteenth-century Britain was alive and well, yet it never took the extreme forms it took in France under Colbert and in Prussia under Frederick the Great.

The consensus among historians today is that the regulations and rules, most of them relics from Tudor and Stuart times, were rarely enforced. As the economy became more sophisticated and markets more complex, the ability of the government to regulate such matters as the quality of bread . . . effectively vanished. The central government was left to control foreign trade, but most other internal administration was left to local authorities. . . . By ignoring and evading rather than altogether abolishing regulations, Britain moved slowly, almost imperceptibly toward a free-market society . . . [but due to control of foreign trade], free trade remained a far cry from reality until well into the nineteenth century. . . . A slow trend toward lower tariffs began in 1825, culminating in the abolition of the Corn Laws in 1846, and the repeal of the Navigation Acts, which had severely limited foreign freighters from carrying British goods, in 1849–1854.

ator of economic growth: "The capital employed in agriculture . . . puts into motion a greater quantity of productive labour than any equal capital employed in manufactures . . . [and] adds a much greater value to the annual produce of the land and labour of the country, to the real wealth and revenue of its inhabitants."[50]

In addition to investments gained from greater trade in agricultural products, British agriculture had benefited since the late 1600s from the habit of wealthy British merchants of retiring to country estates. Economic historian E.L. Jones explains how the boom in mercantile trade affected farm improvements:

Much wealth was generated by the rapid expansion of the export and re-export trades and much of it was invested in the land by the successful merchant class, so great has the social magnetism of a country estate always been to Englishmen. As Josiah Child remarked as early as 1668, "If a merchant in England arrives at any considerable estate [wealth], he commonly withdraws his estate from trade before he comes near the confines of old age." The rich merchant bought a country seat. Agriculture could not but be the gainer from this transfusion of trading capital, allied as it was to new farming practices spreading among a more progress-minded rural community.[51]

NEW FORMS OF TRANSPORT

All the food from the improved farms could not be moved without better transportation. British roads were particularly bad before the 1700s, but a solution was found when Parliament set up small companies to build toll roads, to be paid for through collection of money from users. Defoe described the new system in the 1720s:

> The roads had been plow'd so deep, and materials have been in some places so difficult to be had for repair of the roads, that all the surveyors rates [taxes collected from farmers for road repair] have been able to do nothing; nay, the very whole country has not been able to repair them; that is to say, it was a burthen too great for the poor farmers; for in England, it is the tenant, not the landlord, that pays the surveyors of the highways.

This necessarily brought the country to bring these things to the Parliament; and the consequence has been, that turnpikes or toll-bars have been set up on the several great roads of England, beginning at London, and proceeding thro' almost all of those dirty deep roads, in the midland counties espe-

A vendor brings produce to market along a canal. Throughout the 1700s countries around the world developed canal systems to facilitate the transport of goods.

cially; at which turn-pikes all carriages, droves of cattle, and travellers on horseback, are oblig'd to pay an easy toll; that is to say, a horse a penny, a coach three pence, a cart four pence, a waggon six pence . . . cattle pay by the score, or by the head . . . the benefit of a good road abundantly making amends for that little charge the travellers are put to at the turn-pikes. [52]

In contrast to the often poor condition of roads, transportation by water was always good around the boundaries of the British Isles, and across the channel to the rest of Europe. Inside England, however, only the Severn River was navigable for cargo. After 1760, a kind of canal-building mania set in, in imitation of the Dutch, who had been using canals for a hundred years before that. The first British canals were created by private companies made up of people looking for cheaper ways to move products such as coal. Soon a very busy national canal system was transporting everything from china to chickens. William Cobbett took note of the canals but doubted they were helping rural people. He wrote:

> I saw in one single farmyard here, more food than enough for four times the inhabitants of the parish; and this yard did not contain a tenth, perhaps, of the produce of the parish; but, while the poor creatures that raise the wheat, the barley, and cheese, and the mutton, and the beef, are living upon potatoes, an accursed *Canal* comes kindly through the parish to convey away the wheat, and all the good food to the tax-eaters and their attendants in the Wen [city]! I could

broom-stick the fellow who would look me in the face and call this "an improvement." [53]

Elsewhere in Europe, canal systems were built about the same time. In France and Germany, canal building was paid for by the Crown, sometimes more for prestige and glory than for profit making. The grand French canal connecting the Mediterranean with the Atlantic, the Canal des Deux Mers, attracted almost no international traffic and was closed through most of the 1700s because it needed repairs.

The impressive canal system of the United States was funded by individual states, where farmers had great political influence. Farmers were solidly behind the canals because getting anything to market was so difficult. Roads were very poor or nonexistent west of the Appalachian Mountains—and distances were great. The best way to move goods was by water, on rivers or on lakes. A canal system promised to connect the rivers and lakes with the interior, where so many people were trying to farm. Canal building began with the Erie Canal, connecting Albany and Buffalo in 1825. The canals allowed wonderful savings of time and money, connecting inland farmers with the Great Lakes and the Ohio and Mississippi river systems. Canals helped cities grow all over the world, such as Birmingham in central England and Akron in the American Midwest.

STEAM TRANSPORTATION

In the nineteenth century, steam was applied to transportation, and it greatly increased

A steamship enters San Francisco harbor. Steamships stimulated commerce by lowering the cost of transportation of goods.

markets and made trade less expensive. Again, the story began in Britain because the inventors of the steam engine were there. Steamships began to ply rivers and oceans in the 1820s. Journalist Henry Mayhew described the busy London docks at midcentury:

> As you enter the dock, the sight of the forest of masts in the distance, and the tall chimneys vomiting clouds of black smoke, and the many coloured flags flying in the air, has a most peculiar effect. . . . The sailors are singing . . . songs from the Yankee ship just entering, the cooper is hammering at the casks on the quay, the chains of the cranes, loosed of their weight, reel as they fly up again. . . . Here the heavily laden ships are down far below the quay, and you descend to them by ladders, whilst in another basin they

are high up out of the water, so that their green copper sheathing is almost level with the eye of the passenger; while above his head a long line of bowsprits stretches far over the quay, and from them hang spars and planks as a gangway to each ship. [54]

The great volume of trade the ships carried was matched by the capacity of the railroad train. The first public railway line opened between Liverpool and Manchester, England, in 1830, and within twenty years, railways were all over the world. Trains brought the usefulness of canals to an end, although barge traffic on rivers remains important today for agricultural products. The train carried the products of the agricultural revolution into the new era of fully developed industry.

5 Social Effects of the Agricultural Revolution

The agricultural revolution brought about great changes in people's lives, though it occurred at different times in different places. For the British, the new agriculture meant an end to many things that had seemed unchangeable since medieval times, including periodic famine, the ties between a lord and his people, and the way of life in common fields villages. For some people, this move toward a more modern world was good; but for others, it was wrenching. The social problems accompanying the changes were themselves new and ways of handling them had yet to be invented.

IMPROVED FARMS AND AMBITIOUS FARMERS

The people who immediately benefited most from the agricultural revolution in Britain were large landowners and tenant farmers holding relatively large farms. Arthur Young, promoter of the Norfolk four-course system, said:

> All the country from Holkham to Houghton was a wild sheepwalk before the spirit of improvement seized the inhabitants, and this glorious spirit has wrought amazing effects: for instead of the boundless wilds and uncultivated wastes inhabited by scarce anything but sheep, the country is all cut into enclosures, cultivated in a most husbandlike manner, richly manured, well peopled, and yielding a hundred times the produce that it did in its former state. . . . [Enclosure has] changed the men as much as it has improved the country. . . . When I passed from the conversation of the farmers I was recommended to call on, to that of men whom chance threw my way, I seemed to have lost a century in time, or to have moved 1,000 miles in a day. . . . He, who is the Best Farmer, is with me the Greatest Man.[55]

Young noted that the newly prosperous tenant farmers were beginning to act like gentlemen, buying pianos and carriages, sending their children to boarding schools and even university. Young did not approve, because he had old-fashioned ideas about social class, but he could not overlook the change.

In some parts of England, the fever of improvement led tenant farmers to make such intensive use of the land that even landowners were alarmed. An agent in the county of Hampshire remarked, "The tenant is too much disposed to sow the land in a greater proportion than it ought to be; it would pay her better if less of the Down land were in tillage."[56] In 1810, an agricultural surveyor in the same area declared that those who plowed previously uncropped land were full of "madness, extravagance, and folly."[57] But the chances taken on the new methods most often turned out to be worth it, at least in terms of profit.

Profit, in fact, became the most valuable thing to farmers' lives. Leisure was less approved than in the past, for a variety of reasons. The number of holidays was steadily decreasing, and landlords no longer were expected to provide large festivals. Hard

Tenant farmers, like this group, who adopted the new farming methods often became wealthy as a result of the increased productivity of their land.

work, furthermore, could result in a surplus that could be sold—something not always possible in the past. The churches of England, influenced by reformers, taught the virtue of work. A parson in 1825 reflected the feeling that farm life had become less cheerful and more focused on profit, "the acquirement of property":

It may be said that the present generation compared with the former is dull and selfish and that the cheerfulness which once was found among them seems for ever banished from the place. To this I would reply that the [low level] of the people's wants occasioned in earlier times but little care and called forth less exertion. A small population in a large domain required but easy labour to procure the simple necessities of life. This was all they attempted or all they desired. . . . The levity of "bygone days"

A small farmer uses a horse-drawn plow during the 1800s. Small farmers worked their land with tremendous industry, but their yields were substantially smaller than those of large farmers.

hath in modern times assumed the form of a more dignified demeanour and those moments which where spent by past generations in useless inactivity are by the present employed in providing for more than their daily wants and those of their families. The consequence of which is . . . that the present compared with the former race of villagers are advanced in the scale of intellect and increased in the acquirement of property.[58]

SMALL FARMERS

Small farmers in Britain at this time were perhaps even less cheerful and certainly made less profit than the large farmers. In the 1600s, most small freehold or tenant farmers could make a good living from less than fifty acres. But they could not produce enough surplus to compete with larger farms. Furthermore, enclosure meant the small farmer was no longer entitled to use common pastures once held by the community as a whole, which had partly solved farmers' need for more space. The large farmer also had the advantage in economy of scale. Both the small and the large farmer needed a team of horses, for instance. But the large farmer could use his to plow several times the acreage of the small farm. The small farmer still had to pay the same price for his team, but his yield was much lower. At the time of enclosure, tenants did their best to combine farms and create the largest they could afford for this reason. Arthur Young wrote, "I regard these small occupiers as a set of very miserable men. They . . .

work without intermission like a horse . . . without being able to soften their present lot."[59] Another observer, the Reverend John Howlett, noted that constant work kept the small farmer even from learning how to improve his life:

> The small farmer is forced to be laborious to an extreme degree; he works harder and fares harder than the common labourer; and yet with all his labour and with all his fatiguing constant exertions, seldom can he at all improve his condition or even with any degree of regularity pay his rent and preserve his present situation. He is confined to perpetual drudgery, which is the source of profound ignorance, the parent of obstinacy and blind perseverance in old modes and old practices, however absurd and [harmful].[60]

It is not surprising that the number of small-farm families declined through the 1800s.

THE GREATEST VICTIMS

The changes associated with the agricultural revolution had the greatest impact on the lives of villagers who owned or rented little or no land. Under the old common fields system, village families could keep themselves alive in a variety of ways. They could keep a garden around their cottage. They could pasture a few animals of their own on the commons. They could hunt or trap in certain places and gather wood, nuts, berries, and herbs from the local woods. They could practice a craft at home, such as basket making, and barter items and jobs with nearby neighbors. New laws and enclosure, however, tended to sweep all that away.

Hunting in most forests was made illegal for everyone but the wealthy before 1700. The Game Law of 1671 permitted hunting only by owners of farms worth more than one hundred pounds, or leaseholds worth more than 150 pounds. Nobody else was allowed to hunt, even on their own property. Meanwhile, six men invited to a shooting party by a wealthy landowner could easily kill three thousand game birds in one weekend. Wood-gathering in the forest remained legal in many places, but feeling grew against it. An argument of great influence was made by Sir Frederic Mortimer Eden at the end of the 1700s. The poor, he said, do not budget money for fuel:

> Nothing is stated for fuel. If the labourer is employed in hedging he is allowed to take home a faggot [bundle of wood] every evening, while the work lasts; but this is by no means sufficient for his consumption: his children, therefore, are sent into the fields, to collect wood where they can, and neither hedges nor trees are spared by the young marauders who are thus, in some degree, calculated in the art of thieving, till, from being accustomed to small thefts, they hesitate not to commit greater deprivations on the public. [61]

Gleaning, the process of gathering remaining grain from fields after the harvest, was also made illegal. Landowners began to argue that gleaners were trespassers with no real right on the land. They were stealing the produce that belonged to the owner. A Suffolk case, approved in court, claimed the biblical law was not valid:

> The law of *Moses* is not obligatory on us. It is indeed agreeable to Christian charity and common humanity, that the rich should provide for the impotent poor, but the mode of such provision must be of positive institution. We have established a nobler fund. We have pledged all the landed property of the kingdom for the maintenance of the poor, who have in some instances exhausted the source. [62]

This legalistic view was reinforced by brisk, efficient, usually wealthy people like one Mr. Ruggles, who said: "How many days, during the harvest, are lost by the mother of a family and all her children, in wandering about from field to field, to glean what does not repay them in wear and tear of their cloaths in seeking?" [63] Some historians have named this process of removing old common rights the "custom to crime" transition. It reflected a new reverence for private property.

ENCLOSURE AND AGRICULTURAL WAGE WORK

In the process of enclosure, the wealthier villagers moved out to their own farmlands, and often the village itself fell into decay. William Cobbett noted this with horror:

> Here are new enclosures without end. And there are new houses too, here and there, over the whole of this execrable

Villagers such as these women who did not own land would often gather the remaining grain from harvested fields, a practice known as gleaning.

tract of country. . . . But farm-houses have been growing fewer and fewer; and it is [clear] to every man who has eyes to see with, that the villages are regularly wasting away. . . . In all the really agricultural villages and parts of the kingdom, there is shocking decay, a great dilapidation and constant falling down of houses. . . . The labourers' houses disappear also. . . . If this infernal system could go on for forty years longer, it would make all the labourers as much slaves as the Negroes are.[64]

Cobbett was writing in the period following the Napoleonic Wars, when grain prices had fallen to very low levels; but still, the plight of the landless villager was hard. Some found work as hired laborers on the larger farms, where big teams of men were

A LABORER TRIES TO GET BY

In the deep winter of 1850 an impoverished agricultural worker named Cooper Lawson sat down to write to the steward of the landholder of his area. He asked not for an increase in his pay, but for the chance to do work at home that might supplement his income. Cooper's letter shows the pride, the sad poverty, and lack of education of workers on the land at that time. His letter is reproduced in J.D. Chambers and G.E. Mingay, The Agricultural Revolution: 1750–1880.

December 11, 1850

Kind Gentulman: i hope you will pardon my bouldness in aproching so grate a nobility. i ashure you it is distress that causes me to do it. i am a labering man with a famely of smal children. i am working for sixteen pens a day. i am paying 2 shilens a week for rent, 1 shiling for coal, so that you see that their is very littel for our liveing. i have 2 hours at a night that i have nothing to do and if you will be so kind to give me a bit of ling [brush, a kind of heather] from Skillingthorp i can spend my time at night in making besoms [brooms] which whould bring me in a littel, theirfore i hope that by the blessing of God and your kindness i shal be able to provide things honist in the sight of all men.

i am your humbel servant, Cooper Lawson,
Waddington, near Lincoln

needed especially for harvest. Even an employed laborer could have trouble finding a home, however, as old village land was taken as someone's private farm. Laborers traveled by foot, sometimes for many miles, to get to work.

Conditions of labor varied, but in general they were spare. The diet of an agricultural laborer on the Salisbury Plain was described this way in 1851:

> After doing up his horses he takes breakfast, which is made of flour with a little butter, and water "from the tea kettle" poured over it. He takes with him to the field a piece of bread and (if he has not a young family, and can afford it) cheese to eat at mid-day. He returns home in the afternoon to a few potatoes, and possibly a little bacon, though only those that are better off can afford this. The supper very commonly consists of bread and water. The appearance of the labourers showed, as might be expected from such meagre diet, a want of that vigour and activity which mark the well-fed ploughman.[65]

While some employers provided housing and tiny plots for potato growing, the trend was toward a strictly wage-based exchange. A commentator of the mid-1800s remarked on the difference between old-fashioned farming in the north and the modern Norfolk system: "After the elaborate, and, we may almost say, paternal methods pursued in the north, the Norfolk system of labour is not very attractive. There is no such thing as a yearly labourer, no boarding [food] paid for by the farmer, and, in short, no connection between master and man except work on the one hand and payment on the other."[66] Especially in hard times, the wage of an agricultural laborer was barely enough to keep him alive.

The wives and children of agricultural laborers did not fare better. Some joined groups of thirty to forty women and children hired by gang bosses beginning in the 1820s. A gang would be let out to a farmer to do weeding and other farm chores by the day. No housing or food had to be provided by the farmer. The gangs camped out and cooked for themselves. The evils of this system for the workers included physical hardship, abuse, and lack of education for children.

An Irish family waits to board a ship for America. The depressed wages of nineteenth-century agricultural laborers in Europe forced many to immigrate to the New World, Australia, and Africa.

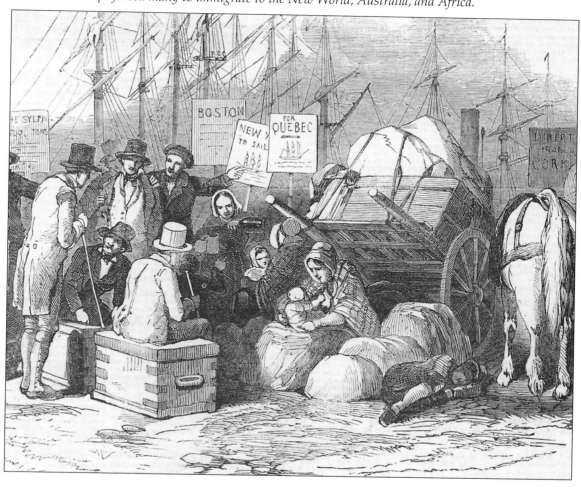

A final alternative for some rural people was immigration. While going to Australia or North America was a good solution for many families, critics such as Oliver Goldsmith worried that with enclosure and "improvement," the backbone of Britain, its peasantry, was being forced off the land. In a very popular poem of 1770, "The Deserted Village," he drew this picture:

> Sweet smiling village, loveliest of the
>   lawn,
> Thy sports are fled and all they
>   charms withdrawn;
> Amidst thy bowers the tyrant's hand
>   is seen,
> And desolation saddens all thy green:
> One only master grasps the whole do-
>   main,
> And half a tillage stints thy smiling
>   plain:
> No more thy glassy brook reflects the
>   day,
> But, choked with sedges, works its
>   weedy way.
>
> And, trembling, shrinking from the
>   spoiler's hand,
> Far, far away, thy children leave the
>   land.
> Ill fares the land, to hastening ills a
>   prey,
> Where wealth accumulates and men
>   decay:
> Princes and lords may flourish or may
>   fade;
> A breath can make them, as a breath
>   has made;
> But a bold peasantry, their country's
>   pride,
> When once destroyed, can never be
>   supplied. [67]

THE POOR LAWS

Farmworkers' lives were strongly affected by the Poor Laws of Britain, which provided aid to the very needy. By law as of 1700, this "relief" was provided by each parish, based on a tax on the land. Traditionally, poor relief included support for the old, sick, or disabled in their own homes; finding work for the able-bodied who needed it; and getting apprenticeships for children. In practice, the Poor Laws generally did a poor job of all three; but they were strengthened by the fatherly attention of wealthy landowners, who felt responsible for their people. It was customary for lords' wives, for instance, to visit the poor and ill of the parish with gifts and medicines.

The old Poor Laws were complicated by another law that made the parish responsible only for people legally "settled" within its boundaries. This law tended to keep poor workers within the parish; but when enclosure or other changes made them lose their cottages, they were no longer eligible for relief. Farmers often deliberately tore down cottages on their land so they would not have to pay high poor taxes.

In 1795 the town of Speenhamland began a new system that added to workers' wages from the poor taxes, on a flexible scale based on the price of bread. The idea was an old-fashioned, paternal one: that all the people should be provided for. The system spread through many British parishes. In practice, though, it only made matters worse. Farmers felt free to offer even lower wages than before. Workers felt no need to work hard, since they would receive full pay whatever they did.

THE CRAZE FOR GIN

In 1690 Britain's Parliament passed "An Act for encouraging the distilling of brandy and spirits from corn." The idea was to create a new market for British grain, and farmers were behind it. Yet the act led to the making of vast amounts of distilled juniper-flavored Geneva spirits, popularly nicknamed "gin." Before Parliament recognized the problem of alcoholism and reversed the law in the mid-1700s, Londoners in particular suffered from this effort to help the farmer. A report of 1726 is reproduced in Patrick Dillon's Gin: The Much-Lamented Death of Madam Geneva.

Go along the streets, and you shall see every brandy shop swarming with scandalous wretches, swearing and drinking as if they had no notion of a future state. There they get drunk by daylight, and after that run up and down the streets swearing, cursing and talking beastliness like so many devils; setting ill examples and debauching our youth in general. . . . Young creatures, girls of 12 and 13 years of age, drink Geneva [gin] like fishes, and make themselves unfit to live in sober families . . . and they talk enough to make a man shudder again; there is no passing the streets for 'em, so shameless are they grown. . . . New oaths are coin'd every day; and little children swear before they can well speak. . . . Geneva is now grown so general a liquor that there is not an ale-house . . . but can furnish you with a dram of Gin.

POPULATION AND THE NEW POOR LAW

It became clear over the course of the 1700s that more and more of the people living in the countryside were agricultural wage workers. Some people argued that enclosure had driven these people away from home villages and forced them to become a mobile labor force. Others said the population was growing rapidly, and there were more workers because more people were surviving childhood. Probably both were true. In any case, alarm was certainly increasing over the rising numbers of truly impoverished rural people. Thomas Malthus, in *An Essay on the Principle of Populations* (1798), said that

population growth threatened to lead to famine. Food production, he argued, increased arithmetically: 2, 4, 6, and so on. Population, on the other hand, increased by multiples: 2, 4, 16, and so on. This apparently scientific approach convinced many people who were already worried about the expense of keeping the poor. The logical conclusion was that people who could not support themselves should be discouraged from having families, and should if possible be forced to work.

With these thoughts in mind, Parliament passed a new Poor Law in 1823. This law swept away the Speenhamland system, the settlement law, and the last of the old Poor Laws. Instead, it concentrated relief in the workhouse, a way of handling the poor, which was first established in Britain in the 1720s. The workhouse was a kind of boardinghouse where work was required of the able-bodied. Workhouses were made deliberately unpleasant. Families were required to separate on entering a workhouse, and food was very poor and sparse. One parson, visiting a Norfolk workhouse in 1781, remarked, "About 380 Poor in it now, but they don't look either healthy or cheerful, a great Number die there, 27 have died since Christmas last."[68]

The new Poor Law reflected the ideas that each individual should be responsible for his or her welfare, should work in order to receive benefit, and should not be tied to the landowner or the land itself. The British Poor Law may seem harsh—and it seemed so to many British people of the time. Yet it was more generous than those of many other European countries And, by separating relief from the land, it encouraged workers to leave the land and the lord and to seek work wherever they could find it. Historian Mark Overton claims that "The English poor law encouraged the growth of wage labor, the decline of servants and the growth of farm sizes."[69] Meanwhile, the threat Thomas Malthus raised worried people into the twentieth century. It was a long while before it became evident that food production had easily kept up with population growth. The predicted famines never took place.

PROTESTS

The changes in the British countryside did not go on without protest. Food riots had occurred in the past, when harvests failed and grain was scarce and expensive. In the 1700s and early 1800s, however, famine was not the issue. Instead, people were protesting changes in the agricultural system, which they felt were harming their lives. In general, the protesters wanted to restore old ways and customs. In 1756–1757, for example, farmers attacked middlemen and corn dealers, who they thought were cheating them. In the 1790s, there were riots against price-fixing on the part of grain merchants. There had been some riots opposing enclosure in the 1600s, but parliamentary enclosure did not attract much active unrest. The reason was probably the fact that Parliament permitted citizens to petition against a bill of enclosure: there was a built-in way to object. Of course, only landowners had a voice in that process.

By far, the greatest rural protests of the period were the "Captain Swing" riots of 1830–1831. Probably motivated by a sudden drop in farm wages, the rioters protested enclosure in general, low wages, the employment of "strangers," and the farm machines (chiefly threshing machines) that were keeping people out of work. All over England, gangs of people gathered, often with blackened faces and in women's clothing, to burn down ricks and barns, smash machinery, and cut down fences. They sent threatening letters, such as this one: "This is to inform you what you have to undergo Gentelmen if providing you Don't pull down your messhenes and raise the poor man's wages the married men give tow and six pence a day the singel tow shillings or we will burn down your barns and you in them this is the last notis."[70] Often, the letters were signed with the fictional name, "Captain Swing."

Farm laborers were at the heart of the Captain Swing riots, but tenant farmers also took part in some places. In Sussex, a woman reported on a meeting in the local church:

> I am ashamed to say the farmers encouraged the laboring classes who required to be paid 2s.6d. [two shillings and sixpence] a day, while the farmers called for a reduction in their rents and tithes by one half. . . . Mr. Hurst held out so long that it was feared blood would be shed. The doors were shut till the demands were granted; no lights were allowed; the iron railing that surrounds the monument was torn up, and the sacred boundary between the chancel and alter overleaped before he would yield; at last the three points were gained &

A mob of English farmworkers burns down a farm in 1830. During that year, farmworkers rioted to protest depressed wages and the use of farm machines.

happily without any personal injury. . . . Money was afterwards demanded at different houses for refreshment &, if not obtained with ease, the windows were broken. Today the mob is gone to Shipley and Rusper.[71]

If the British government had treated the rioters harshly, and ignored their problems, the Captain Swing riots might have led to much worse violence. As it was, the British government created special commissions to hear all voices and to conduct the trials of the accused. Only a few people died in the rioting, and only nineteen protesters out of many hundreds arrested were executed (mostly for arson). The worst sentence (after execution) was transportation: five hundred and five people were sentenced to travel to British colonies, to begin a new life.

FACTORY GIRLS WRITE HOME TO THE FARM

The textile mills at Lowell, Massachusetts, were some of the first factories in the United States. They employed young women aged fifteen to twenty-two, nearly all of them from farm families. While critics said the factory life would be hard and would have a bad effect on the girls, letters collected in Thomas Dublin's Transforming Women's Work *suggest that the mill gave the girls new freedom, independence, and income that was much needed.*

"I am not living upon my friends or doing housework for my board but am a factory girl. . . . I want to see you very much but am making good wages now and if I go home I see no way of earning anything through the spring. . . . I did not mind you when you wished me to leave the mill. We were making such good pay that I wanted to work a little longer."
- Anna Mason

"I shall need all I have got and as for marrying and settling in that wilderness I wont. And if a person ever expects to take comfort it is while they are young I feel it so."
- Sally Rice

"I have earned enough to school me awhile, & have not I a right to do so, or must I go home, like a dutiful girl, place the money in father's hands, & there goes all my hard earnings. . . . I merely wish to go to Oberlin [college] because I think it the best way of spending the money I have worked so hard to earn."
- Lucy Ann

"And now Mother I am going to propose a plan that we Lowell folks have formed, which is, that I stay here all winter, and go home in the spring, and then I shall not feel obliged to come back again for a year. . . . My reasons for this are, first, I am here *now* and *very pleasantly situated,* which is a good deal for factory girls to say, and I think if I am going to work in Lowell any more, I had better stay now."
–Sarah Metcalf

They joined a good number of voluntary refugees from rural Britain who were already farming in the abundant lands of the Americas, Australia, or Africa.

FROM FARM TO FACTORY

Hard-pressed farm laborers could and did look for better work and a better life elsewhere. Immigration was just one alternative. For many people, the obvious choice was a job in industry, or in the steadily growing commercial world where industrial goods were bought and sold. Industrial work was not strange to the English countryside because much industry got its start there. Since medieval times, town merchants had "put out" work to rural villagers, who made lace or wove wool or hammered nails, and sent the products to the merchant for a little pay. This cottage industry increased during the early 1700s in areas where most agriculture was pastoral (raising sheep or cows), particularly in the midlands and north. The rhythm of work in crop-raising areas made cottage industry less profitable there. As machinery and organization of workers in factories developed, using water power or steam power, it was natural for the owners to draw upon the workers who had done similar work at home. That is one reason why British industry was concentrated in the midlands and north, in such cities as Birmingham, Manchester, and Leeds.

The history of the British industrial revolution is full of accounts of the terrible conditions in the new factories: long hours of boring, repetitive work; dangerous working conditions; and ugly surroundings. Yet in the middle of the 1800s, an industrial worker in Britain made just over twice what a farm laborer earned. In a novel of the day, *North and South,* British writer Elizabeth Gaskell contrasted industrial work in the north with agricultural work in the south of the country. At one point, an unemployed industrial worker, age forty-four, considers going south to seek work on a farm. The heroine argues against it with reasons that are historically correct:

> "But what kind of work could you do, my man?"
>
> "Well, I reckon I could spade a bit—"
>
> "And for that," said Margaret, stepping forward, "for anything you could do, Higgens, with the best will in the world, you would, may be, get nine shillings a week; may be ten, at the outside. . . . You must not go to the South. . . . You could not stand it. You would have to be out in all weathers. It would kill you with rheumatism. The mere bodily work at your time of life would break you down. The fare is far different to what you have been accustomed to."
>
> "I'se not particular about my meat," said he, as if offended.
>
> "But you've reckoned on having butcher's meat once a day, if you're in work; pay for that out of your ten shillings, and keep those poor children if you can. . . . You would not bear the dulness of the life; you don't know what it is; it would eat you away like rust. . . . The hard spadework robs [laborers'] brains of life; the sameness of their toil deadens their imagination; they don't care to meet and talk over thoughts and

speculations . . . after their work is done. . . . You could not stir them up into any companionship which you get in a town as plentiful as the air you breathe, whether it be good or bad."[72]

One reason the industrial worker would find the farmworker dull was that far fewer farmworkers could read. One study shows over half of farmworkers illiterate, while less than a fifth of workers in metals and textiles could not read in the mid-1800s. Factory workers and city dwellers had more chances to gain skills, to make more money, and to advance in life. The number of farmworkers in England peaked in 1851, and had reduced measurably by 1861—even though agricultural output increased. A commentator on that census said he could "only conclude that the redundant [extra] agricultural population has been absorbed by manufacturing industry; and that those who remain are more efficient, better paid, and more fully employed than they were ten years ago."[73]

CHANGES OUTSIDE BRITAIN

In the rest of Europe, more extreme social turmoil accompanied changes in agricultural villages and the growth of industrial work. A wave of revolutions across Europe in 1848 generally failed, but national governments were put on notice that the working people demanded a voice and reform was needed. In Russia the extreme economic and social chasm between the small ruling class and the large toiling poor population led to revolution there in 1905.

The case in North America was different largely because of the existence of the West, which continued to accomodate needy and unhappy people as well as ambitious and adventurous people through the end of the first decade of the 1900s. Farmers before the Civil War enjoyed prosperity in many places, but they became more dependent on the growing commercial and industrial systems to lend them money, to carry and consume their goods, and to make products (like farm machinery), which they now could not do without. Historian David B. Danbom points out that farmers of the time have been labeled "irrational" because by the mid-1800s investments in farming returned only half the profits of the same investments in industry. However, he says:

> There was no shortage of people who wanted to acquire farms. Whatever its shortcomings, farming still promised a higher degree of individual independence and family security than urban occupations offered. And the farmer was still celebrated as the prototypical American and the most perfect representative of all that was good about the country.[74]

THE CITIES "INCREASE THAT PRODUCE"

British cities, home to most industry and commerce, were fed by a flood of food produced by the agricultural revolution. By 1800 London was the largest city in Europe, with a population of about a million. The next largest European city, Paris, held only

DIRE PROBLEMS IN LONDON

In his book London: A Social History, *Roy Porter quotes London officials who reported on the dreadful conditions in which poor people were living in the rapidly expanding city in the early nineteenth century. These areas were often the first addresses for laborers from the country seeking work in the city. The fact that reports were written suggests attention to the problems if not immediate improvements.*

From *Appendix to the Fifth Annual Report of the Poor Law Commissioners* (1839):

These neglected places are out of view and not thought of; their conditions are known only to the parish officers and the medical men whose duties oblige them to visit the inhabitants to relieve their necessities and to attend to the sick; and even these services are not to be performed without danger. During the last year, in several of the parishes, both relieving officers and medical men lost their lives in consequence of the brief stay in these places which they were obliged to make in the performance of their duties.

From a report by City Medical Officer of Health John Simon (1848):

Let the educated man devote an hour to visiting some very poor area in the metropolis. Let him fancy what it would be to himself to live there, in that beastly degradation of stink, fed with such bread, drinking such water. . . . Let him talk to the inmates, let him hear what is thought of the bone-boiler next door, or the slaughter-house behind; what of the sewer-grating before the door; what of the Irish basket-makers upstairs—twelve in a room, what of the artisan's dead body, stretched on his widow's one bed, beside her living children.

about half that many people. Furthermore, England was the most urbanized country in Europe, with many small cities and towns. About a quarter of the British populace lived in towns of over five thousand people.

The towns all grew with the increase in farm produce, industry, trade, and better transportation. London alone drew an estimated eight thousand young people in 1700, who went there to seek their fortunes. Many more were doing the same a hundred years

later. The influx into the cities brought with it some unexpected effects. For instance, town guilds, which had for centuries policed standards for craftsmen, fell apart as the nature of the work changed, and market forces of prices and wages helped determine how work was done. At the same time, banks were created, replacing old groups of financiers who once met in coffeehouses. In London, citizens took to the streets to protest everything from weavers' pay to Irish immigration to gin taxes. As the poor increased in number, so did crime in the streets. Handling pollution and sewage became a tremendous job. The cities struggled to manage growth, make laws, and find solutions to these problems, which often took decades and sometimes proved impossible.

Despite such complications of growth, London in particular became a tremendous national engine, both taking in products and sending out profit to make more products. Daniel Defoe described the effect:

This whole kingdom are employed to furnish something, and I may add, the best of everything, to supply the city of London with provisions, corn, flesh, fish, butter, cheese, salt, [fuel], timber, etc., and cloths also, with every thing necessary for building, and furniture for their own use, and for trade . . . [and] as

Workers load corn onto Spanish ships for export. By 1850 the agricultural revolution had helped create a global economy based largely on the trade of excess farm goods.

every part of the kingdom sends up hither the best of their produce, so they carry back a return of wealth; the money flows from the city into the remotest parts, and furnishes them again to increase that produce, to improve the lands, pay rent to their landlords, taxes to their governors, and supply their families with necessaries: and this is Trade. [75]

London and the other cities of Britain lay at the heart of a new interconnected, rapidly growing economic and social web. And by 1850 other cities around the world were also growing and changing because of the new agriculture. In the United States, for example, New York mushroomed largely because it lay at the mouth of the Hudson River, connected by then via the river, the Erie and other canals, and the Great Lakes to the vast mid-American farmlands. In New York farm goods were transferred from canal barges to steamship holds and distributed around the world. The cities were far from the villages and fields where the agricultural revolution began. But they showed clearly by the mid-1800s what a powerful change that revolution had helped bring about.

Epilogue

Far-Reaching Consequences of the Agricultural Revolution

The agricultural revolution is a piece of world history with many complicated and surprising consequences. Just two examples from the end of the revolution help show how it influenced major world events.

AMERICAN SLAVERY REVIVED, THEN DEFEATED

The expansion, and then the end, of slavery in the United States are both due in some measure to the agricultural revolution. The invention of the cotton gin by Eli Whitney in 1793 led to an enormous expansion of slavery in the United States, as cotton plantations spread across the Appalachians and all the way to the Mississippi River. It is perhaps strange that the cotton gin, part of the great American technological contribution to the agricultural revolution, should lead to a kind of farming far from the advanced methods coming into use elsewhere. In fact, plantation farming most resembled the serf-farmed estates of Russia. There, vast lands were being farmed by forced labor. The owners grew rich in both places by selling their product—Russian grain, or American cotton—on the world market.

When the first slaves were brought to the Americas, few people objected. In fact, no church officially opposed slavery before 1750. Yet as the period continued, Enlightenment and capitalist ideas about the rights and dignity of the individual gained ground. The principle was famously embodied in the American Declaration of Independence, issued July 4, 1776: "We hold these truths to be self-evident: that all men are created equal, endowed by their Creator with certain inalienable rights." Enlightenment philosopher John Locke had earlier carried the idea further, to the notion that each man had a right to the fruits of his own labor: "Though the Earth, and all inferior Creatures be common to all Men, yet every Man has a *Property* in his own Person. This no Body has any Right to but himself. The *Labour* of his Body, and the *Work* of his Hands, we may say, are properly his."[76]

The concept that workers own their labor is part of a basic principle of capitalism, namely that workers should be free to sell their labor wherever they wish. Masters are not responsible for their workers beyond paying them, and workers are free to move anywhere in search of the best wages. This idea gained so much strength between 1700 and 1850 that it was regarded as a moral truth and was used to argue for the abolition of slavery. In the new states of the American West, where there was a clear choice to be made between slave labor and free, outraged advocates of free labor spoke out, as in this newspaper notice of 1860:

> The Missouri Republican State Central Committee in its late address says: There are now in Missouri at least fifty thousand men who cannot get full employment for their energies and enterprise, owing to the depression of the last two years, and there are now in Missouri more than one hundred thousand slaves, occup[y]ing and filling the most lucrative [profitable] agricultural and mechanical positions of the interior. It is the demand of the Republican party that slave labor shall make room for free white labor, and take itself away.[77]

Thus, the principle of a mobile labor force, so important a part of the agricultural revolution, helped to defeat the plantation system when the Civil War finally led to the end of slavery in the United States in 1865.

An abolitionist speaks at an antislavery meeting in Boston. The need for a mobile and free labor force in the United States helped to bring an end to the institution of slavery.

However, as the article suggests, "free white labor" was more eager to find jobs for itself than to deal with the problems of the slavery system or its remains. After the Civil War, there were voices calling for real change. For example, a black school principal, Francis L. Cardozo, spoke to the South Carolina constitutional convention in 1868, arguing that "we will never have true freedom until we abolish the system of agriculture which has existed in the Southern States."[78] But the fact is that the former slaves did not become either landowners or a mobile labor force—not until much later in history. Instead, in the sad aftermath of the Civil War, many of them were forced to become sharecroppers on the old plantations, giving part of their crops to landlords while they struggled to survive on the remainder. American abolitionist Frederick Douglass wrote:

> He who can say to his fellow-man, "You shall serve me or starve," is a master and his subject is a slave . . . . Though no longer a slave, he is in a thralldom grievous and intolerable, compelled to work for whatever his employer is pleased to pay him, swindled out of his hard earnings by money orders redeemed in stores, compelled to pay the price of an acre of ground for its use during a single year, to pay four times more than a fair price for a pound of bacon and to be kept upon the narrowest margin between life and starvation. . . . When the serfs of Russia were emancipated, they were given three acres of ground upon which they could live and make a living. But not so when our slaves were emancipated. They were sent away empty-handed, without money, without friends and without a foot of land on which to stand."[79]

In the West and parts of the North, some former slaves joined free white workers in finding new homes and new work; but free labor remained only a dream on the old plantations for many decades.

THE IRISH POTATO FAMINE

Potatoes were one of the new crops from the Americas that helped put an end to famine across Europe and permitted populations to

A young boy picks cotton in 1935. After the Civil War, many freed slaves had no option but to continue working on cotton plantations as sharecroppers.

Landowners distribute clothing to victims of the Irish potato famine. Starvation forced mass migration from Ireland and fueled anger at British colonial government.

grow. In Ireland after 1846, though, those very qualities spelled doom for the Irish.

Ireland was officially part of Britain in the mid-1800s, but in fact most good farmland was owned by wealthy Protestant landlords of English heritage. Their tenant farmers and farmworkers were generally native Irish Catholics. Most grain on these farms was grown for export to England, where it fetched a good price. The Irish workers survived on a diet that depended very heavily on potatoes. Small farmers, many of them in the west of Ireland, were raising sizeable families on as little as one acre of potatoes.

In 1845 much of the Irish potato crop turned black and rotted. No one knew the nature of the problem: Was it a disease, a drainage problem, or something else? Potatoes that seemed sound were replanted. But they actually held a fungus that was harming the potatoes, in a dormant state. The crop of 1846 was a catastrophic failure. Poor families had nothing to eat and could not afford to buy food at rising prices. They became vulnerable to diseases, and they overflowed the hospitals. Overwhelmed, local parishes could not help, and the British government was not quick with aid. An Irish reporter wrote in the *Times* of Dublin in March 1846:

> Unsound potatoes have bred typhus. The sick are in some cases quintupled; contagion is fearful, even the word we

fear to write—cholera is apprehended. Why is this? Where is it to end? . . . The [British] plans [for relief] were faultless, the scheme of the campaign against the double foe of famine and pestilence was without a flaw. [British prime minister] Sir Robert Peel assures us he has foreseen all that was to happen, but how many are they who have gone to the grave through the wards of the hospitals while he and his colleagues were quarreling and pondering, resigning and resuming office?[80]

Sir Robert Peel did try to relieve the Irish, arranging to send cornmeal to the island, an interesting substitution of one cheap New World food for another. But the aid was inadequate, and later British leaders were not so generous. Some of them claimed that no help should go to Ireland because government aid violated the principles of free market capitalism. That was the system they had embraced because of its apparent success in British agricultural and industrial growth. To the Irish, though, that attitude seemed heartless and cruel, a final blow from long-hated English overlords. The potato famine rekindled Irish nationalism and helped lead eventually to independence for most of the island.

In the meantime, about a million Irish died in the famine and hundreds of thousands immigrated to Britain, Australia, Canada, and especially the United States. Large numbers died in transit, on board the "coffin ships" that carried them. But many made it, and found new lives, even though they arrived in extreme poverty.

The potato famine eased in the 1850s, as villages emptied out. The blight remained a danger, however, until it was discovered that copper sulfite could stop it, in 1882. The potato famine proved that "miracle" crops are not always reliable. It also showed that social and political arrangements, not technological advances, finally determine who gets fed in any era of history.

Notes

Introduction: "Sowing Modernity"

1. Peter D. McClelland, *Sowing Modernity: America's First Agricultural Revolution*. Ithaca, NY: Cornell University Press, 1997, n. p.

2. Jared Diamond, *Guns, Germs, and Steel: The Fates of Human Societies*. New York: W.W. Norton, 1999, p. 89.

Chapter 1: Traditional Farming in Europe

3. Robert Zaller, *Europe in Transition: 1660–1815*. Lanham, MD: University Press of America, 1984, p. 25.

4. Quoted in Keith Wrightson, *Earthly Necessities: Economic Lives in Early Modern Britain*. New Haven, CT: Yale University Press, 2000, p. 63.

5. Quoted in George F. Rudé, *Europe in the Eighteenth Century: Aristocracy and the Bourgeois Challenge*. Cambridge, MA: Harvard University Press, 1972, p. 32.

6. Quoted in Hans-Werner Goetz, *Life in the Middle Ages*, ed. Steven Rowan, trans. Asbert Wimmer. Notre Dame, IN: University of Notre Dame Press, 1993, p. 118.

7. J.D. Chambers and G.E. Mingay, *The Agricultural Revolution: 1750–1880*. New York: Schocken, 1966, p. 23.

8. Quoted in Dorothy Hartley, *Lost Country Life*. New York: Pantheon, 1979, p. 75.

9. Quoted in Deborah Valenze, *The First Industrial Woman*. New York: Oxford University Press, 1995, p. 35.

10. Quoted in Valenze, *The First Industrial Woman*, p. 29.

11. Quoted in Chambers and Mingay, *The Agricultural Revolution*, p. 37.

12. Quoted in Hartley, *Lost Country Life*, p. 63.

13. Quoted in Mark Overton, *Agricultural Revolution in England: The Transformation of the Agrarian Economy: 1500–1850*. Cambridge: Cambridge University Press, 1996, p. 135.

Chapter 2: New Crops and New Methods

14. Quoted in Jonathan Bell and Mervyn Watson, *Irish Farming: 1750–1900*. Edinburgh: John Donald, 1986, p. 114.

15. Herman J. Viola and Carolyn Margolis, *Seeds of Change: Five Hundred Years Since Columbus*. Washington, DC: Smithsonian Institution Press, 1991, p. 52.

16. Quoted in Joan Thirsk, *English Peasant Farming: The Agrarian History of Lincolnshire from Tudor to Recent Times*. London: Methuen, 1981, p. 177.

17. Quoted in Overton, *Agricultural Revolution in England*, p. 110.

18. Daniel Defoe, *A Tour Through the Whole Island of Great Britain*, 1724–1726, vol. 2. Reprint, New York: Dutton Everyman's Library 1962, p. 89.

19. Defoe, *A Tour Through the Whole Island of Great Britain*, p. 97.

20. Quoted in Bell and Watson, *Irish Farming*, p. 25.

21. Quoted in Overton, *Agricultural Revolution in England*, p. 91.

22. Quoted in Overton, *Agricultural Revolution in England*, p. 92.

23. Quoted in Roy Porter, *The Creation of the Modern World: The Untold Story of the British Enlightenment*. New York: W.W. Norton, 2000, p. 303.

24. Quoted in Zaller, *Europe in Transition*, p. 28.

25. Rudé, *Europe in the Eighteenth Century*, p. 25.

26. Quoted in Rudé, *Europe in the Eighteenth Century*, p. 28.

27. Peter Kalm, *Peter Kalm's Travels in North America: The English Version of 1770*. Ed. Adolph B. Benson. New York: Dover, 1987, p. 307.

Chapter 3: Technology Speeds the Revolution

28. Quoted in Wayne D. Rasmussen, *Readings in the History of American Agriculture.* Urbana, IL: University of Illinois Press, 1960, pp. 13–14.

29. Quoted in Chambers and Mingay, *The Agricultural Revolution,* p. 172.

30. Noah Blake, *Diary of an Early American Boy,* ed. Eric Sloane. 1805. Reprint, New York: Wilfred Funk, 1961, pp. xx, 54, 55, 57, 60.

31. William Cobbett, *William Cobbett's Illustrated Rural Rides: 1821–1832.* Exeter, UK: Webb and Bower, 1984, p. 29.

32. Quoted in McClelland, *Sowing Modernity,* pp. 107–108.

33. Quoted in Chambers and Mingay, *The Agricultural Revolution,* p. 71.

34. Quoted in McClelland, *Sowing Modernity,* p. 41.

35. Quoted in McClelland, *Sowing Modernity,* p. 176.

36. Quoted in McClelland, *Sowing Modernity,* p. 210.

37. Quoted in McClelland, *Sowing Modernity,* p. 214.

38. McClelland, *Sowing Modernity,* pp. 62–63.

39. Quoted in Rasmussen, *Readings in the History of American Agriculture,* pp. 69–71.

40. Quoted in Rasmussen, *Readings in the History of American Agriculture,* pp. 78–79.

41. Quoted in Rasmussen, *Readings in the History of American Agriculture,* p. 50.

42. Quoted in McClelland, *Sowing Modernity,* p. 218.

Chapter 4: Landholding and Marketing Transformed

43. Quoted in Porter, *The Creation of the Modern World,* p. 392.

44. Quoted in Overton, *Agricultural Revolution in England,* p. 167.

45. Quoted in James Deetz and Patricia Scott Deetz, *The Times of Their Lives: Life, Love, and Death in Plymouth Colony.* New York: W.H. Freeman, 2000, p. 79.

46. Quoted in T.C.W. Blanning, ed., *The Short Oxford History of Europe: The Eighteenth Century: 1688–1815.* New York: Oxford University Press, 2000, p. 103.

47. Quoted in Digital History, "The South's Economy," *Online American History Textbook.* www.digitalhistory.uh.edu/database/article_display.cfm?HHID=654.

48. Quoted in Overton, *Agricultural Revolution in England,* p. 144.

49. Cobbett, *William Cobbett's Illustrated Rural Rides,* pp. 198–99.

50. Adam Smith, *An Inquiry into the Nature and Causes of the Wealth of Nations.* 1776. Reprint, New York: Modern Library, 1937, p. 345.

51. E.L. Jones, *Agriculture and the Industrial Revolution.* New York: John Wiley and Sons, 1974, p. 88.

52. Defoe, *A Tour Through the Whole Island of Great Britain,* pp. 118–19.

53. Cobbett, *William Cobbett's Illustrated Rural Rides,* p. 169.

54. Quoted in Roy Porter, *London: A Social History.* Cambridge, MA: Harvard University Press, 1995, pp. 189–90.

Chapter 5: Social Effects of the Agricultural Revolution

55. Quoted in Porter, *London,* p. 309.

56. Quoted in Jones, *Agriculture and the Industrial Revolution,* p. 31.

57. Quoted in Jones, *Agriculture and the Industrial Revolution,* p. 54.

58. Quoted in Thirsk, *English Peasant Farming,* p. 297.

59. Quoted in Christopher Hibbert, *The English: A Social History 1066–1945.* New York: Norton, 1987, p. 320.

60. Quoted in Hibbert, *The English,* p. 321.

61. Quoted in Valenze, *The First Industrial Woman,* p. 39.

62. Quoted in Valenze, *The First Industrial Woman,* p. 36.

63. Quoted in Valenze, *The First Industrial Woman,* p. 37.

64. Quoted in Hibbert, *The English,* p. 488.

65. Quoted in Chambers and Mingay, *The Agricultural Revolution,* p. 140.

66. Quoted in Overton, *Agricultural Revolution in England,* p. 185.

67. Quoted in Roger Lonsdale, ed., *New Oxford Book of Eighteenth-Century Verse.* Oxford: Oxford University Press, 1989, p. 524.

68. Quoted in Hibbert, *The English,* p. 493.

69. Overton, *Agricultural Revolution in England,* p. 188.

70. Quoted in Hibbert, *The English,* p. 490.

71. Quoted in Hibbert, *The English,* p. 491.

72. Elizabeth Gaskell, *North and South.* 1854–1855. Reprint, New York: Penguin, 1970, pp. 381–82.

73. Quoted in Jones, *Agriculture and the Industrial Revolution,* pp. 219–20.

74. David B. Danbom, *Born in the Country: A History of Rural America.* Baltimore, MD: Johns Hopkins University Press, 1995, p. 85.

75. Quoted in Porter, *London,* p. 136.

Epilogue: Far-Reaching Consequences of the Agricultural Revolution

76. Quoted in Porter, *The Creation of the Modern World,* p. 187.

77. "How Slaves Drive Out Free Labor," *Repository and Transcript* (Franklin County, PA), August 8, 1860, in *The Valley of the Shadow: Two Communities in the American Civil War,* Virginia Center for Digital History, University of Virginia, http://valley.vcdh.virginia.edu.

78. Quoted in "Proceedings of the Constitution Convention of South Carolina (1868)," *Online American History Textbook,* Digital History, www.digitalhistory.uh.edu/black_voices/voices_display.cfm?id=83.

79. Frederick Douglass, *Life and Times of Frederick Douglass.* Boston: n.p., 1892, *Online American History Textbook,* Digital History, www.digitalhistory.uh.edu/black_voices/voices_display.cfm?id=86.

80. *Times (Dublin),* "The Apprehended Scarcity," March 20, 1846, The Irish Famine 1846–50, University of Virginia, www.people.virginia.edu/~eas5e/Irish/Delay.html.

For Further Reading

Susan Campbell Bartoletti, *Black Potatoes: The Story of the Great Irish Famine: 1845–1850.* New York: Houghton Mifflin, 2001. This story is well told, illustrated with black-and-white engravings, and enlivened with many first-person accounts.

Jake Goldberg, *Food: The Struggle to Sustain the Human Community.* New York: Franklin Watts, 1999. This history of food production around the world includes the period of the agricultural revolution and places it in global context.

Roger Hart, *English Life in the Eighteenth Century.* New York: G.P. Putnam's Sons, 1970. A beautifully illustrated book, with many firsthand sources; the chapter "Life in the Provinces" discusses farming and provincial towns.

Kathryn Hinds, *Life in the Middle Ages: The Countryside.* New York: Benchmark/Marshall Cavendish, 2001. The stunning illustrations in this book help explain European village-centered farming, which was not much changed by the 1600s.

R. Douglas Hurt, *American Farm Tools: From Hand-Power to Steam-Power.* Manhattan, KS: Sunflower University Press, 1982. A survey of the important developments and inventions in American farm tools before the invention of diesel and gasoline engines, including period illustrations and historic photographs.

Sylvia A. Johnson, *Tomatoes, Potatoes, Corn and Beans: How the Foods of the Americas Changed Eating Around the World.* New York: Athenaeum, 1997. New World foods in Europe are only part of this full and entertaining account, illustrated with archival pictures.

Derek Nelson, *The American State Fair.* Osceola, WI: MBI, 1999. A history and a current account of state fairs across the United States, including information about historic reenactments of early farm practices; fully illustrated.

Roy Sturgess, *The Rural Revolution in an English Village.* Cambridge: Cambridge University Press, 1981. This modest British book is a useful study of changes in a village due to the agricultural and industrial revolutions.

R.J. Unstead, *Emerging Empire: A Pictorial History: 1689–1763.* Morristown, NJ: Silver Burdett, 1972. Here is a good explanation of mercantilism and its connection with the British Empire as well as with farm practices; many illustrations.

Works Consulted

Books

Jonathan Bell and Mervyn Watson, *Irish Farming: 1750–1900*. Edinburgh: John Donald, 1986. Focused on implements and techniques rather than human stories, this book nonetheless tells the story of potato cultivation and the scientific basis of the potato famine in Ireland.

Noah Blake, *Diary of an Early American Boy*. Ed. Eric Sloane. 1805. Reprint, New York: Wilfred Funk, 1961. A delightful, true diary, with detail added by Sloane. Illustrated with original drawings of early American tools and methods used on Blake's farm.

T.C.W. Blanning, ed., *The Short Oxford History of Europe: The Eighteenth Century: 1688–1815*. New York: Oxford University Press, 2000. The author makes an excellent case for the impact of the agricultural revolution on European population growth, and sees it as the necessary prequel to modern life.

J.D. Chambers and G.E. Mingay, *The Agricultural Revolution: 1750–1880*. New York: Schocken, 1966. Though an older book, this account of the agricultural revolution in Britain is thorough and includes many wonderful quotations.

A.C. Chibnall, *Sherington: Fiefs and Fields of Buckinghamshire Village*. Cambridge: Cambridge University Press, 1965. Thorough tabulation of the owners and tenants of property in an English village over several centuries.

William Cobbett, *William Cobbett's Illustrated Rural Rides: 1821–1832*. Exeter, UK: Webb and Bower, 1984. Like Daniel Defoe but a century later, Cobbett covered the British countryside and commented on everything; his is a lively but often prejudiced voice. Illustrated with works of the time.

David B. Danbom, *Born in the Country: A History of Rural America*. Baltimore, MD: Johns Hopkins University Press, 1995. A well-written account of the social history of farm life in the United States.

James Deetz and Patricia Scott Deetz, *The Times of Their Lives: Life, Love, and Death in Plymouth Colony*. New York: W.H. Freeman, 2000. A readable account of the true Pilgrim story, with detail about daily life.

Daniel Defoe, *A Tour Through the Whole Island of Great Britain*. Vol. 2. 1724–1726. Reprint, New York: Dutton Everyman's Library, 1962. Defoe tells the story of his trip on horseback all over England, Wales, and Scotland; his informative account was an early armchair-travel book, and remains pleasant to read.

Jared Diamond, *Guns, Germs, and Steel: The Fates of Human Societies*. New York: W.W. Norton, 1999. This ambitious book tells the story of the beginning of agriculture, how it spread, and what the surprising consequences were.

Patrick Dillon, *Gin: The Much-Lamented Death of Madam Geneva*. Boston: Justin,

Charles, 2003. An entertaining popular account of London's eighteenth-century gin craze.

George Francis Dow, *Everyday Life in the Massachusetts Bay Colony.* 1935. Reprint, New York: Benjamin Bloom, 1967. This book includes especially informative chapters on the colonist farmer and farmhouse.

Thomas Dublin, *Transforming Women's Work: New England Lives in the Industrial Revolution.* Ithaca, NY: Cornell University Press, 1994. Interesting account of positive and negative changes in women's jobs and status during the industrial revolution.

Elizabeth Gaskell, *North and South.* 1854–1855. Reprint, New York: Penguin, 1970. This novel has a melodramatic plot, but the author contrasts agricultural southern England with the industrializing north in an authentic way.

Hans-Werner Goetz, *Life in the Middle Ages.* Ed. Steven Rowan, Trans. Albert Wimmer. Notre Dame, IN: University of Notre Dame Press, 1993. An account of life all over Europe in medieval times; explains feudalism well.

Douglas Harper, *Changing Works: Visions of a Lost Agriculture.* Chicago: University of Chicago Press, 2001. Sociologist Harper interviews rural people of the northern Midwest about changes in farming they experienced.

Dorothy Hartley, *Lost Country Life.* New York: Pantheon, 1979. A compendium of information about British country life and how everything was done before

mechanization, with excellent illustrative drawings and farmers' calendar poems.

Christopher Hibbert, *The English: A Social History 1066–1945.* New York: Norton, 1987. A profilic, popular historian offers an ambitious, highly readable overview of the lives of common folk in Britain from the Norman Conquest to the modern day. Includes a wealth of practical detail on farm life.

Daniel Hurley, *Cincinnati: The Queen City.* Cincinnati, OH: Cincinnati Historical Society, 1982. Colorful history of the southern Ohio city, including description of its role as an animal processing center in the early 1800s.

E.L. Jones, *Agriculture and the Industrial Revolution.* New York: John Wiley and Sons, 1974. This collection of essays includes good treatment of agricultural labor in England.

Peter Kalm, *Peter Kalm's Travels in North America: The English Version of 1770.* Ed. Adolph B. Benson. New York: Dover, 1987. The English translation of the original travel diary of Swedish botanist Peter Kalm, who found much of interest and much to criticize in early American farming.

Roger Lonsdale, ed., *New Oxford Book of Eighteenth-Century Verse.* Oxford: Oxford University Press, 1989. Highly regarded, comprehensive collection of period verse reflecting contemporary issues as well as timeless themes.

Peter D. McClelland, *Sowing Modernity: America's First Agricultural Revolution.*

Ithaca, NY: Cornell University Press, 1997. This book tells the story of the spate of invention of farming implements that followed the War of 1812; with many illustrations from advertisements of the time.

Joel Mokyr, ed., *The British Industrial Revolution: An Economic Perspective.* 2nd ed. Boulder, CO: Westview, 1999. An anthology of critical assessments of the industrial revolution in Britain; a chapter addresses the changing role of agriculture from 1700 to 1860.

Mark Overton, *Agricultural Revolution in England: The Transformation of the Agrarian Economy: 1500–1850.* Cambridge: Cambridge University Press, 1996. An excellent account of the agricultural changes in England, with a wealth of statistics and charts to support it.

Rowland Parker, *The Common Stream: Portrait of an English Village Through 2,000 Years.* New York: Holt, Rinehart, and Winston, 1975. Through court records, tax returns, wills, archaelogical evidence, and oral reminiscence, Parker gives the history of the village of Foxrton, the most thorough account of any village in England.

Roy Porter, *The Creation of the Modern World: The Untold Story of the British Enlightenment.* New York: W.W. Norton, 2000. Excellent explanations of eighteenth-century British thinking, including Enlightenment, individualism, and capitalism, with many lively quotations.

———, *London: A Social History.* Cambridge, MA: Harvard University Press, 1995. An energetic journey through London's history, with good chapters on the city of the eighteenth and nineteenth centuries.

Wayne D. Rasmussen, *Readings in the History of American Agriculture.* Urbana, IL: University of Illinois Press, 1960. This collection of original sources will never be dated, although some of them are dense with technical detail.

George F. Rudé, *Europe in the Eighteenth Century: Aristocracy and the Bourgeois Challenge.* Cambridge, MA: Harvard University Press, 1972. This work is especially good for its pan-European perspective and description of agriculture in various zones of Europe.

Adam Smith, *An Inquiry into the Nature and Causes of the Wealth of Nations.* 1776. Reprint, New York: Modern Library, 1937. This classic of capitalism is long but surprisingly easy to read; a thorough index is included.

A.M.W. Stirling, *Coke of Norfolk and His Friends.* London: John Lane/Bodley Head, 1912. A biography of eighteenth-century British landowner Thomas Coke, well known for his devotion to agricultural improvement.

Joan Thirsk, *English Peasant Farming: The Agrarian History of Lincolnshire from Tudor to Recent Times.* London: Methuen, 1981. A close-up view of agricultural change in one British county, divided by time periods.

Deborah Valenze, *The First Industrial Woman.* New York: Oxford University Press, 1995. This book includes sections on women's work on the farm and how women were affected by enclosure in Britain.

Herman J. Viola and Carolyn Margolis, *Seeds of Change: Five Hundred Years Since Columbus.* Washington, DC: Smithsonian Institution Press, 1991. A fascinating book about American plants used around the world, and about European plants coming to the Americas.

George Washington, *Letters on Agriculture from His Excellency, George Washington, President of the United States, to Arthur Young, Esq., F.R.S., and Sir John Sinclair, Bart., M.P., . . . on the Economy and Management of Farms in the United States.* Ed. Franklin Knight. Philadelphia: W.S. Martien, 1847. Washington details his farming practices and innovations in his correspondence, with statistical tables and comments contributed by Thomas Jefferson and other gentleman farmers of the day.

Keith Wrightson, *Earthly Necessities: Economic Lives in Early Modern Britain.* New Haven, CT: Yale University Press, 2000. Social historian Wrightson traces the influence of social attitudes and values on the emerging market economy in Britain, from 1500 to 1800.

Robert Zaller, *Europe in Transition: 1660–1815.* Lanham, MD: University Press of America, 1984. The author includes an account of French farms and explains why farm improvement was limited in prerevolutionary France.

Internet Sources

Frederick Douglass, *Life and Times of Frederick Douglass.* Boston: n.p., 1892, *Online American History Textbook,* Digital History, www.digitalhistory.uh.edu/black_voices/voices_display.cfm?id=86.

European Food Information Council, "The Origins of Maize: The Puzzle of Pellagra," *Food Today,* EUFIC Online, www.eufic.org/gb/food/pag/food30.food303.htm.

"How Slaves Drive Out Free Labor," *Repository and Transcript* (Franklin County, PA), August 8, 1860, in *The Valley of the Shadow: Two Communities in the American Civil War,* Virginia Center for Digital History, University of Virginia, http://valley.vcdh.virginia.edu.

Mark Overton, "Agricultural Revolution in England, 1500–1850," BBC History, http://www.bbc.co.uk/history/society_culture/industrialisation/agricultural_revolution_01.shtml.

"Proceedings of the Constitution Convention of South Carolina (1868)," *Online American History Textbook,* Digital History, www.digitalhistory.uh.edu/black_voices/voices_display.cfm?id=83.

Digital History, "The South's Economy," *Online American History Textbook.* www.digitalhistory.uh.edu/database/article_display.cfm?HHID=654.

Times (Dublin), "The Apprehended Scarcity," March 20, 1846, The Irish Famine 1846–50, University of Virginia, www.people.virginia.edu/~eas5e/Irish/Delay.html.

Yetholm Village Council, "History of Industry & Employment in the Parish," Yetholm Scotland, Scottish Borders, www.yetholm.bordernet.co.uk/history/industry.html.

Web Sites

A History of American Agriculture, 1776–1990, U.S. Department of Agriculture

(www.usda.gov/history2). This government-sponsored site offers historical overviews of American agriculture via useful timelines.

What You Need to Know About: Agriculture, HistoryNet (http://europeanhistory .about.com/cs/agriculture). Well-chosen collection of links to sites related to the agricultural revolution, from the Cornell University Core Historical Literature of Agriculture archive, to biographies of inventors, to detailed studies of specific crops such as the potato and farm implements such as scythes and threshers.

Index

hemp, 37
holidays, 24, 75
Holland, 10, 32, 37, 46, 65, 68
  canal building by, 71
  landholding systems in, 64
  trade in, 28
  wasteland reclamation in, 36
  see also Netherlands
Homestead Act (1862), 56
Horse Hoeing Husbandry (Tull), 44
horse hoes, 44, 48–49, 56
horsepower, 47–48, 49, 50, 56
horses, 10, 12, 77
Howlett, John, 77
Hudson River, 91
hunting, 78
Hussey, Obed, 57

immigration, 82, 86–87, 96
imports, 68
  see also trade
incomplete proteins, 12
increase vendible, 64
industrial revolution, 45–46, 53, 59, 87
  see also technology
inheritance laws, 16
inventions, 49–51, 52–54
  see also technology
Ireland, 30, 38
  inheritance laws in, 16
  potato famine in, 94–96
irrigation, 22
Italy, 20, 29, 30, 40, 41, 64

Jefferson, Thomas, 51–52, 53
Jones, E.L., 69–70

Kent, Nathaniel, 61–63
kings, 15

landholding systems, 10

changes in, 60–66
technology impact on, 45
Lawson, Cooper, 80
Leeds (England), 87
leisure, 75–77
lentils, 11
lime, 38
Lincolnshire (England), 32
Linearbrandkeramik culture, 12
literacy rates, 88
Liverpool (England), 73
loans, 68
Locke, John, 38, 92
London (England), 88–91
London Corn Exchange, 67
lord of the manor, 61, 63, 64–65, 74, 82
Louisiana Territory, 53
Louis XIV (king of France), 41
Low Countries, 15, 32, 36, 41
Lowell, Francis C., 58

Madison, James, 51
maize, 11, 29, 40
see also corn
Malthus, Thomas, 83, 84
Manchester (England), 73, 87
mangels, 32
manors, 15, 20, 24
  see also lord of the manor
manure, 12, 25, 26, 34, 36, 38
Marboef, Marquess of, 64
marketing system, 60, 66–70
markets, 26–27, 45, 67, 68
Markham, Gervase, 17
marl, 38
marshes, 36–37
Massachusetts, 58, 63
Mayhew, Henry, 72–73
May-weed, 23
McClelland, Peter D., 10, 54
McCormick, Cyrus, 57
McCormick reaper, 49, 57

Meikle, Andrew, 50
mercantilism, 68, 69–70
Mesoamerica, 10
Mesta, 25
Mexico, 10, 40
middlemen, 27, 67–68, 84
Mississippi River, 71
Moses (biblical figure), 23–24, 78

Nancy (France), 51
Napoleonic Wars, 79
Native Americans, 12–13
Navigation Acts, 69
Netherlands, 15, 32
  see also Holland
Newcomen, Thomas, 58
New Leicester sheep, 36
Newton, Isaac, 38
New York, 91
nitrogen, soil, 26, 32
noblesse oblige, 63
Norfolk system, 36, 38, 41, 74
  introduction of, 32–34
  social effects of, 80–81
North America, 29, 82
  landholding systems in, 63–64
  social changes in, 88
  unimproved farms in, 42–43
  see also Americas
North and South (Gaskell), 87–88
Northwest Territory, 52–53

oats, 21, 23, 34, 45
Ohio River, 71
Overton, Mark, 84
oxen, 21, 46, 47

paring and burning, 38
Paris (France), 88–89
patents, 54
Paul, Lewis, 58

Picture Credits

About the Author

Cathryn J. Long studied literature at the University of California, Berkeley. She writes nonfiction books for young people in areas of civics, history, and world affairs. Her other books for Lucent include *Ancient America* and *The Cherokee*. She is also a writer and researcher for a University of Cincinnati project that allows people to virtually visit ancient Indian earthworks through a computer-generated landscape.